Orpheus

A Lyrical Legend

[The allusions in this poem to classical legend or myth are too numerous to be dealt with by annotation. A good dictionary will enable the reader to trace all the allusions]

Aleister Crowley

Copyright © 2012 A Mystical World Reprints

All rights reserved.

ISBN-10:1482381451

ISBN-13: 978-1482381450

CONTENTS

                                            Page

Orpheus –

CONTENTS	1
WARNING	4
EXORDIUM	5
LIBER PRIMUS VEL CARMINUM	8
LIBER SECUNDUS VEL AMORIS	54
LIBER TERTIUS VEL LABORIS	80
LIBER QUARTUS VEL MORTIS	128

Aleister Crowley

CONTENTS.

WARNING.
THE POET: EXORDIUM.

BOOK I.

Introductory Ode --
  Str. α Calliope.
  Ant. α Orpheus.
  Str. β Calliope.
  Ant. β Orpheus.
  Str. γ Calliope.
  Ant. γ Orpheus.
  Epode Calliope.

Str. α Orpheus in alternate invocation.

Ant. α The Elemental Forces --

  Semichorus α Lightning.
      "   β Volcanoes.
  Chorus -- Fire.
  Semichorus α Winds.
      "   β Clouds.
      "   γ Mist.
      "   δ Rain.
      "   ε Frost.
      "   ζ Snow.
      "   η Ice.
      "   θ Dew.
      "   ι Hail.
      "   κ Rainbow.
  Chorus -- The Tempest.
  Semichorus α Fountains.
      "   β Lakes.
      "   γ Torrents.
      "   δ Rivers.
      "   ε Waterspouts.
      "   ζ Eagre.
      "   η Wells.
      "   θ Bays.
  Chorus -- The Sea.
  Massed Semichorus α of Earth-Spirits.
  Massed Semichorus β of Living Creatures of Earth.
  Chorus -- The Earth.

Str. β Orpheus in alternate invocation.

Anto. β Time --

  Semichorus α The Hours.
      "   β The Seasons --

Semichorus α Spring.
    " β Summer.
    " γ Autumn.
    " δ Winter.
Semichorus γ The Years.
    " δ The Lustres.
        Spirit .
        Air : In harmony   ⎫ In harmony
        Water : developing ⎬ developing
        Earth : the five-   ⎨ the five-
        Fire . fold idea.   ⎭ Fold idea
Semichorus ε The Centuries.

                          ⎧ α Centuries
                Semichorus ⎨ β Mahakaplas
                          ⎩ γ Manwantaras
                               δ Eternity

Str. γ Orpheus

Ant. γ Death --
    (Suppressed antistrophe, Death being silent. His reply is really given in Books II., III., IV.)

Parabasis: The poet.

Epode: Nature.

BOOK II.

Orpheus laments his wife -- *"come back, come back, come back, Eurydice."*
    "Fling down the foolish lyre, the witless power."
Complains of the antithesis of desire and power -- *"Let the far music of*
    oblivious years."
Laments - *"How can one hour dissolve a year's delight."*
Tells of his wooing -- *"In child-like meditative mood."*
Eurydice's song -- *"O shape half seen of love, and lost."*
Continues the tale of his wooing – *"Such tune my failing body snapped."*
Invokes Aphrodite -- *"Daughter of Glory, child."*
Continues the tale of his wooing -- *"I caught the lavish lyre, and sate."*
Eurydice's song -- *"Who art thou, love, by what sweet name I quicken."*
Continues the tale of his wooing -- *"So by some spell divinely drawn."*
Orpheus' song -- *"Roll, strong life-current of these very veins."*
Concludes his lament -- *"So sped my wooing: now I surely think."*

BOOK III

Orpheus recounts his journey to Hades -- *"As I pass in my flight."*
Invokes the guardians -- *"Hail to ye, wardens."*
Continues his voyage -- *"The phantoms diminish."*
Invokes Hecate -- *"O triple form of darkness! Sombre splendour!"*
Continues his voyage -- *"The night falls back."*
Trio: Minos, Æacus, Rhadamanthus -- *"Substantial, stern, and strong."*

Orpheus

Orpheus' plea -- *"O iron, bow to silver's piercing note!"*
Trio: Minos, Æacus, Rhadamanthus -- *"Brethren, what need of wonder."*
Orpheus continues his voyage -- *"Ah me! I find ye but ill counsellors."*
Invokes Hades -- *"Now is the gold gone of the year, and gone."*
Invokes Persephone -- *"In Asia, on the Nysian plains, she played."*
Persephone awakes -- *"Ah me! I feel a stirring in my blood."*
Orpheus pleads with her -- *"And therefore, O most beautiful and mild."*
Persephone invokes Hades -- *"Ah me! no fruit for guerdon."*
Orpheus invokes the Furies -- *"In vain, O thou veiled."*
Septet: The Furies, Orpheus, Hades, Persephone, Echidna -- *"Ha! who invokes? What horror rages."*
Orpheus invokes Hermes -- *"O Light in Light! O flashing wings of fire!"*
Orpheus' song of triumph -- *"The magical task and the labour is ended."*
Continues to recount his journey -- *"So singing I make reverence and retire."*
Sings his triumph -- *"O light of Apollo."*
Sings, but with misgiving -- *"Alas! that ever the dark place."*

BOOK IV.

Company of Mænads -- *"Evoe! Evoe Ho! Iacche! Iacche!"*
Song -- *"Hail, O Dionysus! Hail."*
"'Evoe Ho! Give me to drink.'"
Hymn to Dionysus -- *"Hail, child of Semele."*
"He is here! He is here!"
Dionysus -- *"I bring ye wine from above."*
Mænads -- *"O sweet soul of the waters! Chase me not."*
Orpheus his spell -- *"Unity uttermost showed."*
His allocution -- *"Worship with due rite, orderly attire."*
His hymn to Pan -- *"In the spring, in the loud lost places."*
His alarm -- *"What have I said? What have I done?"*
Lament for Orpheus -- Quartet: a Spirit, the River Hebrus, Calliope, the Lesbian Shore -- *"What is? what chorus swells."*
Sappho's song -- *"Woe is me! the brow of a brazen morning."*
Duet: Calliope, the Lesbian Shore -- *"Silence. I hear a voice."*
Finale. Nuith -- *"Enough. It is ended, the story."*

Aleister Crowley

WARNING.

MAY I who know so bitterly the tedium of this truly dreadful poem be permitted to warn all but the strongest and most desperate natures from the task of reading or of attempting to read it? I have spent more than three years in fits of alternate enthusiasm for, and disgust of, it. My best friends have turned weeping away when I introduced its name into conversation; my most obsequious sycophants (including myself) were revolted when I approached the subject, even from afar.

I began Book I. in San Francisco one accursed day of May 1901. I was then a Qabalist, deeply involved in ceremonial magic, with a Pantheon of Egypto-Christian colour, in fact, the mere bouillon of which my "Tannhauser" was the froth. The idea was to do the "biggest thing ever done in lyrics." I bound myself by an oath to admit no rhyme unless three times repeated; to average some high percentage of double rhymes -- in brief, to perform a gigantic juggle with the unhappy English language. The whole of this first book is technically an ode (!!!) and was so designed. So colossal an example of human fatuity truly deserves, and shall have, a complete exposure.

Book I. was finished in Hawaii, ere June expired, and Book II. begun.

I had just begun to study the Theosophic writings -- their influence, though slight, is apparent. So intent was I on producing a "big" book that the whole of my "Argonauts" was written for the shadow-play by which Orpheus wins Eurydice to an interest in mortal joys and sorrows. Also -- believe it! -- I had proposed a similar play in Book III., to be called "Heracles" or "Theseus," by performance of which Persephone should be moved, or Hades overwhelmed.

But luckily I was myself overwhelmed first, and it never got a chance at Hades. Book II., then, and its Siamese twin, were written in Hawaii, Japan, China, Ceylon, and South India, where also I began Book III. That also I finished in the Burmese jungle and at Lamma Sayadaw Kyoung at Akyab.

During this period I was studying the Buddhist law; and its influence on the philosophy of the poem is as apparent as that of Hinduism on Book II.

The summer of 1902 asked another kind of philosophy -- the kind that goes with glacier travel in the Mustagh Tagh. Orpheus slept.

Book IV. was begun in Cairo on my way to England, and bears marks of confirmed Buddhism up to the death of Orpheus.

But the more I saw of Buddhism the less I liked it, and the first part of Book IV. is flatly contradicted by its climax.

This is a pitiable sort of confession for a man to make!

What was I to do? I could not rewrite the whole in order to give it a philosophic unity. Gerald Kelly forcibly prevented me from throwing it into the river at Marlotte, though he admitted quite frankly that he could not read even through Book I. and did not see how any one could. Tell me, he said, conjuring the friendship of years, can "you" read it? Even a poet should be honest; I confessed that I could not!

Taking it in sections, with relays and an ambulance, we could see no fault in it, however. It is clumsily built; it is all feet and face; but you cannot make a monster symmetrical by lopping at him.

Still, we cut down every possible excrescence, doctored up the remains so as to look as much like a book as possible (until it is examined), and are about to let it loose on society.

The remaining books all share this fatal lack of Architecture; but they are not so long; there is some incident, though not much; and they are proportionately less dull. Further, the scheme is no longer so ambitious, and the failure is therefore less glaring.

Orpheus

I might have done like Burton and his Kasidah, and kept the MS. for twenty years (if I live so long), ever revising it. But (*a*) I should certainly not live twenty years if I had the accursed manuscript in all sorts and sizes of type and colour of ink and pencil to stalk my footsteps, and (*b*) I am literally not the man who wrote it, and, despise him as I may, I have no right to interfere with his work.

But I will not be haunted by the ghost of a Banquo that another man has failed to lay; and this kind of ghost knows but one exorcism.

One should bury him decently in fine fat type, and erect nice boards over him, and collect the criticisms of an enlightened press, and inscribe them on the tomb.

Then he is buried beyond resurrection; oblivion takes him, and he will never haunt the author or anybody else again.

Old Man of the Sea, these three years you have drummed your black misshapen heels upon me; I have had no ease because of you; I am bepissed and conskited of your beastliness; and now you are drunk with the idea that you are finished and perfect, I shall roll you off and beat your brains out upon that hardest of flints, the head of the British Public. I am shut of thee. Allah forget thee in the day when he remembereth his friends!

August 14, 1904.

EXORDIUM.

FROM darkness of fugitive thought,
  From problems bewildering the brain,
Deep lights beyond heaven unsought,
  Dead faces seen dimly in rain;
    From the depths of Mind's caverns, the fire
    Reclaims the old magical lyre;
The ways of creation are nought,
If only, O mother, O Muse, I may measure Thy melodies in me again!

How wayward, how feeble the child
  Three watched from the stars at his birth;
Erato the fierce and the mild;
  Polymnia grave; and the girth
    Broad-girdled of gold and desire,
    Melpomene's terrible lyre,
That lifts up her life in the wild,
The star-piercing paean, and floats in mid-ether, and sinks to the earth.

These three of the Muses were mine;
  They nurtured and knew me and kissed.
Erato was hidden in wine;
  Polymnia dawned in the mist:
    Melpomene shone in the pyre
    Of terrors that burned in her lyre;
But all of their passion divine
I lost in the life and the stress of the world ere ever the soul of me wist.

But, Orpheus, thy splendider light
  Was the veil of thyself the more splendid.

Aleister Crowley

Thou leapedst as a fountain in flight,
As a bird in the rainbow descended!
From the sweet single womb risen higher
Did Calliope string thee her lyre,
Thy mother: and veiled her in night: --
For thyself to Herself art a veil till the veils of the Heaven be rended and ended.

Now, single myself as thy soul,
I pray to Apollo indeed!
Fling forth to the starriest goal
My spirit, invoking his rede;
Care nought for his mercy or ire;
Reach impious hands to his lyre.
Determined to die or control
Those strings the immortal at last, though the strings of this heart of me bleed.

Come life, or come death; come disdain
Or honour from mutable men,
I cry in this passionate pain --
My blood be poured out in the pen!
Euterpe! Espouse me! inspire
My life looking up to Thy lure!
Of thy love, thine alone, am I fain!
Be with me, possess me, reveal me the melodies never yet given to men.

The starry and heavenly wheels,
The earth and her glorious dye,
The light that the darkness reveals,
The river, the sea, and the sky;
All nature, or joyful or dire,
Life, death, let them throng to the lyre,
All sealed with the marvellous seals!
Let them live in my sob, let them love in my song, let them even be I!

Let me in most various song
Be seasons, be rivers that roll,
Be stars, the untameable throng,
All parts of the ultimate whole;
All nature in various attire
Be woven to one tune of the lyre,
One tune where a million belong --
Multitudinous murmur and moan, melodious, one soul with my soul!

One soul with the wail of distress
The ravished Persephone flung;
One soul with the song of success,
Demeter's, that found her and sung;
One soul with all spirits drawn nigher
From invisible worlds to the lyre; --
They throng me and silently press
The strings as I need them, and quicken my fingers and loosen my tongue!

And thou, O supreme, O Apollo!

Orpheus

I have lived in Thy lands for a year,
Under skies, where the azure was hollow,
The vault of black midnight was clear.
   Think! I who have borne Thee, nor tire --
   May I not lift up on Thy lyre
Most reverent fingers, and follow
Thy path, take Thy reins, drive Thy chariot and horses of song without fear?

Let the lightning be harnessed before me,
   The thunder be chained to my car,
The sea roll asunder that bore me,
   The sky peal my clarion of war!
   As a warrior's my chariot shall gyre!
   As a lord I will sharpen the lyre!
The stars and the moon shall adore me,
Not seeing mean me, but Thyself in the glory, the splendidest star.

Around me the planets shall thunder,
   And earth lift her voice to the sea;
The moon shall be smitten with wonder,
   The starlight look love unto me.
   Comets, meteors, storms shall admire,
   Be mingled in tune to my lyre,
The universe broken in sunder, --
And I -- shall I burn, pass away? Having been for a moment the shadow of Thee!

Aleister Crowley

LIBER PRIMUS VEL CARMINUM

TO

OSCAR ECKENSTEIN,
WITH WHOM I HAVE WANDERED IN SO MANY SOLITUDES OF
NATURE, AND THEREBY LEARNT THE WORDS AND
SPELLS THAT BIND HER CHILDREN

Τάχα δ' ἐν ταῖς πολυδένδροισιν Ὀλύμπου
Θαλάμαις, ἔνθα ποτ' Ὀρφεὺς κιθαρίζων
ξύναγεν δένδρεα μούσαις, ξύναγεν θῆρας ἀγρώτας.
—Βάκχαι.

> Orpheus with his lute made trees,
> And the mountain tops that freeze
> Bow themselves when he did sing.
> To his music plants and flowers
> Ever sprung, as sun and showers
> There had made a lasting spring.
>
> Everything that heard him play,
> Even the billows of the sea,
> Hung their heads, and then lay by.
> In sweet music is such art,
> Killing care and grief of heart --
> Fall asleep, or hearing die.
> -- *Henry VIII.*

> ... vocalem temere insecutae
>   Orphea sylvæ,
> Arte materna rapidos morantem
> Fluminum lapsus, celeresque ventos,
> Blandum et auritas fidibus canoris
>   Ducere quercus.
> -- *Hor. Carm.*, Lib. I. xii.

INTRODUCTORY ODE.

CALLIOPE, ORPHEUS.

Str. α.

CALLIOPE.

IN the days of the spring of my being,
  When maidenly bent I above
The head of the poet, and, seeing
  Not love, was the lyre of his love;
When laurels I bore to the harper,
  When bays for the lyrist I bore,
My life was diviner and sharper,

Orpheus

My name in the Muses was more;
When virgin I came to him stainless,
When love was a pleasure and painless!
What Destiny dreams and discovers
The fragrance men know for a lover's?
Peace turned into laughter and tears,
Borne down the cold stream of the years!

Ant. α.

ORPHEUS.
O mother, O queen may-minded,
  More beauty than beauty may be,
More light than the Sun; I am blinded,
  Sink, tremble, am lost in the sea.
The voice of thy singing descended,
  Rolled round me and wrapped me in mist,
Some sense of thy being, borne splendid;
  I dreamed, I desired, I was kissed.
Some breath from thy music hath bound me;
  Some tune from thy lyre hath found me.
Thy words are as rushing of fire;
  But I know not the lilt of thy lure: --
Thy voice is as deep as the sea;
  Thy music is darkness to me.

Str. β.

CALLIOPE.
Child of Thracian sire, on me begotten,
  Knowest thou not the laughter and the life?
Knowest thou not how all things are forgotten,
  Being with a maiden wife?
How a subtle sense of inmost being
  Wraps thee in, and cuts the world away;
Sight and sound lose hearing and lose seeing,
  All the night is one with all the day?
Hearken to her sighing!
Life droops down as dying,
  Melting in the clasp of amorous limbs and hair;
All the darkening world
Round about ye furled --
  Dost thou know, or, knowing, dost thou care?

Ant. β.

ORPHEUS.
Mother, I have lain, half dead, half slumbering,
  Curtained in Eurydice her hair;
Clothed in serpent kisses, souls outnumbering
  Dewdrops flung in spray through air.
I have lain and watched the night diminish,
  Fade and fall into the arms of day,

Caring not if earth itself should finish,
Caring only if my lover stay;
Listening to her breathing,
Laughing, lover-weaving
All the silken gold and glory of her head,
Kissing as if time
Forgot its steeps to climb,
Made eternity's, one with all the dead.

Str. γ.

CALLIOPE.

Listen, then listen, O Thracian!
  Oeager lay on the lea:
I, from my heavenly station;
I, from my house of creation,
  Stopped, as a mortal to be
Passionate, mother and bride;
Flashed on wide wing to his side,
  Caught him and drew him to me.
Kisses not mortal I lavished;
Out of the life of him ravished
  Life for the making of thee,
Son, did I lose in the deed?
Son, did the breasts of me bleed,
  Bleed for pure love? Did I see
Zeus with his face through the thunder
Frowning with fury and wonder?
  Love in Olympus is free --
I have created a god, not a mortal of mortal degree.

Ant. γ.

ORPHEUS.

Hear me, O mother, descended
To earth, from the sisterly shrine!
Hear me, a mortal unfriended,
Save thou, in thy purity splendid
  Indwell me, invoke the divine!
As sunlight enkindles the ocean,
As moonlight shakes earth with emotion,
  As starlight shoots trembling in wine,
So be thy soul for a man!
Teach my young fingers to span
  That musical lyre of thine!
Passion and music and peace,
Teach me the singing of these!
  Teach me the tune of the vine!
Teach me the stars to resemble,
As tide-stricken sea-cliffs to tremble
  Thy strings, as the wind-shaken pine!
Let these and their fruits and the soul of their being be mine, very mine!

Orpheus

EPODE

CALLIOPE

AS the tides invisible of ocean,
  Sweeping under the dark star-gemmed sea;
As the frail Caduceus' serpent-motion
  Moves the deep waves of eternity;
As the star-space lingers and moves on;
As the comet flashes and is gone;
As the light, the music, and the thunder
  Of moving worlds retire;
As the hoarse sounds of the heaven wonder
  When Zeus flings forth his fire;
As the clang of swords in battle;
As the low of home-driven cattle'
As the wail of mothers children-losing;
  As the clamorous cries of darkening death;
As the joy-gasp of love's chosen choosing;
  As the babe's first voluntary breath;
As the storm and tempest fallen at even;
As the crack and hissing of the levin;
As the soft sough of tree-boughs wind-shaken;
  As the fearful cry of souls in hell,
When past death and blinder life they waken,
  Seeing Styx before their vision swell,
When the bands of earth are broken
As the spirit's spell is spoken
On the vast and barren places
  Where the unburied wander still;
As the laughter of young faces;
  As the Word that is the will;
As the life of wells and fountains,
Of the old deep-seated mountains;
As the forest's desolate sighing;
  As the moaning of the earth
Where her seeds are black and dying;
  As the earthquake's sudden birth;
As the vast volcano rending
Its own breasts; as music blending
With young maiden's loving laughter,
  With the joy of fatherhood,
With the cry of Mænads after
  Sacrifice by well or wood;
As the grave religious throng
Moving silently along,
Leading heifers, snowy footed,
  Into glades and sacred groves,
Where the altar-stone is suited
  To commemorate the Loves;
As the choir's most seemly chanting;
As the women's whispers haunting
Silent woods, or chaster spaces,
  Where the river's water wends;

As the sound, when the white faces
  Burn from space, and all earth end.
In the presence of the Gods;
These and all their periods;
These, and all that of them is,
I bestow on thee, and this
Also, mine eternal kiss!
In one melody of bliss
These and thou and I will mingle,
Till all Nature's pulses tingle,
Hear and follow and obey thee,
  Thee, the lyrist; thee, the lyre!
These shall hear and not gainsay thee,
  Follow in the extreme desire,
Mingling, tingling, mixed with thee
Even to all Eternity.
These, and all that of them is,
Take from Calliope in this
Single-hearted, many mouthèd, kiss.

ORPHEUS, SEATED UPON OLYMPUS, TUNES HIS LYRE.

ORPHEUS.

    FIRST word of my song,
      First tune of my lure,
    Muse, loved of me long,
      Be near and inspire!
    Bright heart! Mother strong!
      Sweet sense of desire!
Be near as I lift the first notes impassioned of fervour and fire!

    Not ever before
      Since Nature began
    Hath one cloven her core,
      Found the soul of her span;
    No son that she bore
      Her spirit might scan;
But I, being born beyond Nature, have known her and yet am a man.

    Yet fieriest flowers,
      Life-stream of the world,
    In passionate bowers
      Of mystery curled,
    Come forth! for the powers
      Of my crying are hurled: --
Come forth! O ye souls of the fire, where the sound of my singing is whirled!

    Ye blossoms of lightning,
      Bare boughs of the tree
    Of life, where the brightening

Orpheus

Abysses of sea
Reveal ye, the whitening
Swords kindled of me.
Come forth! I invoke thee, O lightning, the flames of the Gods flung free!

THE LIGHTNING.
The wand of Hermes, the caduceus wonder-working,
Sweeps in mid-æther --
Where we are lurking
It finds us and gathers.
By our mother the amber
In her glorious chamber;
By the flames that enwreathe her;
By the tombs of our fathers;
Awake! let us fly, the compeller is nigh.
Strike! let us die!

ORPHEUS.
Ye powers volcanic,
Cyclopean forces,
Workers Titanic,
I know your courses.
By fury and panic,
By Dis and his horses,
Come forth! I invoke ye, volcanoes, arise from your cavernous sources!

THE VOLCANOES.
The Hephæstian hammer on the anvil of hell,
In the hollows accurst,
Falls for the knell
Of the children of earth.
By the strength of our fires,
The fierce force of our sires,
Let us roar, let us burst!
By the wrath of our birth,
Up! and boil over in rivers of lava!
Uncover! Uncover!

ORPHEUS.
Lit up thine amber
Lithe limber limbs,
Lissome that clamber
Like god-reaching hymns;
The flame in its chamber
Of glory that swims,
The Spirit and shape of the fire, mine eyes with fine dew that bedims!

Exempt from the bond
All others that binds,

Aleister Crowley

As a flowery frond
  The spark of thee blinds,
Within and beyond
  As a thought of the mind's
In all, and about, and above! I invoke thee, my word as the wind's.

THE FIRE.

I, raging and lowering,
I, flying and cowering,
  I, weaving and woven,
Budding and flowering,
Spiring and showering,
  Cleaving and cloven!
My being encloses
Fountains of roses,
  Lilies, and light!
I wrap and I sunder!
I am lightning and thunder!
The world-souls wonder
  At me and my might!

All-piercing, all-winding,
All-moving, all-blinding,
  All shaken in my hissing;
My life's light finding
All spirits, and binding
  Their love with my kissing;
Ruthless, fearless,
Imperial, peerless,
  Creep I or climb.
Nought withstands me,
Bursts me or brands me;
Nor Heaven commands me,
  Nor Space, nor Time.

Above, the supernal!
Below, the infernal!
  Of all am I master.
On Earth, the diurnal!
In all things eternal!
  Life, love, or disaster!
Abiding unshaken,
I sleep and I waken
  On wonderful wings;
In depth and in height,
In darkness and light,
In weakness and might,
In blindness and sight,
in mercy and spite,
In day and in night,
Averse or aright,
For dule or delight,

Orpheus

I am master of things.

ORPHEUS.

O mother, I fear me!
  The might of the lyre!
They tremble to hear me,
  The powers of the fire.
Come near me to cheer me!
  Be near and inspire!
Be strength in my heart and good courage, and speed in the single desire!

The fire knows its master!
  They flicker and flare,
Dread dogs of disaster,
  Wild slaves of despair.
Faster and faster --
  My soul is aware
Of a sound that is dimmer and duller, wide wings adrift of the air.

Their forces that wander
  No God-voice know they!
Their bridals they squander!
  Unknown is their way!
The sky's heart? beyond her
  Sweet bosom they stray.
Shall these then obey me and hear? Shall the tameless one hear and obey?

From secretest places
  Whence darkness is drawn,
Where terrible faces
  Enkindle the dawn,
From wordless wide spaces,
  The ultimate lawn,
Come forth! I invoke thee, O wind, come forth to me fleet as a fawn.

THE WINDS.

From fourfold quarters,
  The depth and the height,
We come, the bright daughters
  of day shed on night;
The sun and the waters
  Have brought us to light;
The sound of him slaughters
  Our soul in his sight.
We hear the loud murmur; we know him; we rest;
  We breathe in his breast.

ORPHEUS.

By sunlight up-gathered
  As dust of his cars,

Aleister Crowley

By moonlight unfathered,
  Unmothered of stars,
Unpastured, untethered,
  Unstricken of scars,
Come forth! I invoke ye, O clouds! ye veils! ye divine avatars!

THE CLOUDS.

Sun's spirit is calling!
  We gather together,
White wreaths, as appalling
  Pale ghosts of dead weather,
The veil of us falling
  On snow-height and heather,
Or hovering and scrawling
  Strange signs in the æther.
We hear the still voice, and we know him we come!
  We are sightless and dumb.

ORPHEUS.

More frail than your friends,
  The clouds borne above,
The light of thee blends
  With the moon and her love.
Thy spirit descends
  As a white-throated dove.
Come forth! I invoke thee, O mist, and make me a sharer thereof!

THE MIST.

From valleys of violet
  My shadow hath kissed,
From low-lying islet,
  A vision of mist,
The voice of my pilot
  Steals soft to insist.
O azure of sky, let
  Me pass to the tryst!
I hear the low voice of my love; and I rest
  A maid on his breast.

ORPHEUS.

Thou child of soft wind
  And the luminous air,
Thou, stealing behind
  As a ghost, as a rare
Soft dew, as a blind
  Fierce lion from his lair,
Come forth! I invoke thee, O rain, look forth with thy countenance fair!

Orpheus

THE RAIN.

From highland far drifted,
From river-fed lawn,
From clouds thunder-rifted,
I leap as a fawn.
The voice is uplifted,
The lord of my dawn;
My spirit is shifted,
My love is withdrawn.
I hear the sweet feet of my God; I know him; I fall
In tears at his call.

ORPHEUS.

Cold lips and chaste eyes
Of frost-fall that leap,
That shake from the skies
On the earth in her sleep
Kiss nuptial, arise
As the lyre-strings sweep!
Come forth! I invoke thee, O frost, the valleys await thee and weep.

THE FROST.

So silent and wise
In her cerement clothes,
So secretly lies
My soul in my snows;
I awake, I arise,
For my spirit now knows
The first time in her eyes
That a voice may unclose
My petals: I hear it; I come; I clasp the warm ground
In my passion profound.

ORPHEUS.

In valleys heaped high,
In drifts lying low,
Swift slopes to the sky,
Come forth to me, snow!
Thy beauty and I
Are of old even so
As lover and lover. Come forth! I invoke thee! the hills are a glow.

THE SNOW.

Bright breasts I uncover,
Heart's heart to thy gaze;
O lyre of my lover,
I know thee, thy praise.
Black heavens that hover,

Blind air that obeys,
I come to thee over
The mountainous ways
As a bride to the bridegroom: I blush, but I come
And bow to thee dumb.

ORPHEUS.

O blacker than hell,
O bluer than heaven,
O green as the dell
Lit of sunlight at even!
O strong as a spell!
O bright as the levin!
Come forth! I invoke thee, O ice, by their anguish, the rocks thou has riven!

THE ICE.

My steep-lying masses,
Mine innermost sheen,
My soundless crevasses,
My rivers unseen,
My glow that surpasses
In azure and green
The rocks and the grasses.
Above, I am queen.
These know thee; I know thee, O master, I hear and obey.
I follow thy lyrical sway.

ORPHEUS.

O tenderest child
And phantom of day!
Gleam fitful and wild
On the flowery way!
Blue skies reconciled
To the kisses of clay!
Come forth! I invoke thee, O dew! The maiden must hear and obey.

THE DEW.

Life trembling on leaves,
Sunrise shed in tears,
Love's arrow that cleaves
The veil of the years,
Light gathered in sheaves
Of tenderest fears
As dayspring enweaves
My soul into spheres --
I hear, and I nestle upon thee, O lyrist supreme,
Light loves in a dream.

ORPHEUS.

Child of sweet rain,
  O fathered of frost!
Bitterest pain
  The birth of thee cost.
Passion is slain
  When wished of thee most.
Come forth! I invoke thee, O hail, thou lord of a terrible host!

THE HAIL.

My father was glad of me
  In places unseen;
My mother was sad of me,
  Where wind came between;
Winter is mad of me,
  Earth is my queen;
Meadows are clad of me,
  Nestled in green.
As pearls in the cloudland I slept; but I hear the loud call;
  I obey it and fall!

ORPHEUS.

Rain's guerdon and daughter
  By sunlight's spies
Divided in water,
  O light-stream, arise!
Seven petals that slaughter
  The menace of Dis,
Come forth! I invoke thee, O rainbow! thou maid of the myriad eyes!

THE RAINBOW.

In multiple measure
  The flowers of us fold
The scarlet and azure
  And olive and gold,
Hyperion his treasure
  Of light that is rolled
In music and pleasure
  Unheard and untold.
We are kisses of light and of tears, love's triumph on fear.
  We obey: I am here!

ORPHEUS.

Dim lights shed around me
  In many a form
Like lovers surround me: --
  O tender and warm!
They hunt me, they hound me;

They struggle and swarm --
Come forth! I invoke ye united, the manifold shape of the storm!

THE TEMPEST.

    Wide-winged, many-throated,
      Colossal, sublime,
    I come and am coated
      With feathers of Time.
    I hear the deep note, head
      My pinions to climb,
    The roar of devoted
      Large limbs of the mime
That mocks the loud lords of Olympus; we mingle; I wake.
    I come with the sound of a snake.

ORPHEUS.

    O storm many-winded,
      O life of the air,
    Thou angry and blinded
      Hast sky for thy share.
    O mother deep-minded,
      My lure to my prayer
Responds, and the elements answer or ever my soul is aware.

    Ye powers of deep water
      And sea-running bays,
    Earth's fugitive daughter
      In deep-riven ways,
    Enamoured of slaughter,
      A mirage of grays,
Deep blues, and pale greens unbegotten, I turn to your lyrical praise.

    I tune the loud lyre
      To the haunts of the vale
    As a sea-piercing fire
      On the wings of the gale.
    I lift my desire,
      I madden, I wail!
Come forth! I invoke ye, O powers, in the waters that purple and pale.

    Come forth in your pleasure,
      O fountains and springs!
    Come dance me a measure
      Unholpen of wings!
    Show, show the deep treasure,
      Unspeakable things!
Come forth! I invoke ye, O fountains, I sweep the invincible strings.

THE FOUNTAINS.

In the heather deeply hidden,
  From the caverns darkly drawn,
In the woodlands man-forbidden,
  In the gateways of the dawn,
In the glad sweet glades descended,
  On the stark hills gathered high,
Where the snows and trees are blended,
  Kissed at birth by sun and sky;
We have heard the summons: we are open to the day-spring's eye.

ORPHEUS.

O broad-bosomed lakes
  Whence the mist-tears uprise,
That shed in sweet flakes
  The gleam of the skies,
Whose countenance takes
  The bird as he flies
In kisses, come forth! I invoke ye, O lakes, where the love of me lies!

THE LAKES.

In the hollow of the mountain,
  In the bosom of the plain,
Fed by river, stream, and fountain,
  Slain by sun, reborn of rain;
In the desert green-engirded,
  Lying lone in waste and wood,
To my breast the many-herded
  Lowing kine in gracious mood
Come, drink deeply, and are glad of me, my pleasant solitude.

ORPHEUS.

From the breast of the snow
  As a life-swollen stream,
Your love-rivers flow
  Soft hued as a dream,
Adrift and aglow
  With the sunlight supreme.
Come forth! I invoke ye, O torrents that fall in the mazes and gleam!

THE MOUNTAIN TORRENTS.

Falling fast or lingering love-wise,
  Gathered into mirror-lakes,
Floating sprayed through heaven dove-wise,
  Dreaming, dashing; sunlight shakes
Into million-coloured petals
  All our limpid drops, and wraps

Earth with green, as water settles
  On the rocks and in their gaps,
Mossy rainbow-tinted maidens, flowers and fernshoots in their laps.

ORPHEUS.

Low down in the hollows
  And vales of the earth,
What eagle-sight follows
  Your length and green girth?
Your light is Apollo's,
  Diana's your mirth!
Come forth! I invoke ye, O rivers, I have watched your mysterious birth!

THE RIVERS.

In the lowland gently swelling,
  Born and risen out of rain,
Wide the curves and arrowy dwelling
  Were we rest or roll again.
There our calm sides shield the mortal,
  Bears his bark our breast, and we
Follow to the mystic portal
  Where we mingle with the sea.
Every life of earth we list to: should not we then answer thee?

ORPHEUS.

O see mixt with æther
  In whirls that awake,
Roar skywards and wreathe her
  Bright coils as a snake,
In agony seethe her
  Sad cries for the sake
Of peace -- I invoke ye! Come forth! O spouts in the wave's wild wake!

THE WATERSPOUTS.

Whirling over miles of ocean,
  Lowering o'er the solemn sea,
Hears our life the deep commotion
  That we know -- thy witchery.
Wheeling, hating, fearing ever
  As we thunder o'er the deep,
Death alone our path can sever,
  Death our guerdon if we weep.
We obey thee, we are with thee! Wilt thou never let us sleep?

ORPHEUS.

O rolled on the river
  By might of the moon,

Orpheus

    Ye tremble and quiver,
    Ye shudder and swoon!
    The cities ye shiver:
    The ships know your tune.
Come forth! I invoke ye, O eagres! dread rivals of shoal and typhoon!

THE EAGRE.

  Flings my single billow spuming
    Into midmost air the world,
  As the echo of my booming
    To the furthest star is hurled.
  Now I hear the lunar clashing
    That evokes me from the tide,
  Now I rise, my fury lashing,
    Rolling where the banks divide --
I obey thee, I am with thee, Lord of Lightning, lotus-eyed!

ORPHEUS.

    In sacred grove,
      In silent wood,
    In calm alcove,
      In mirrored mood,
    What light of love
      Your depth endued?
Come forth! I invoke ye, O wells, ye dwellers of dim solitude!

THE WELLS.

  Deep and calm to heaven's mirror
    Through the cedarn grove or ashen,
  Willow-woven, or cypress terror,
    To the sky's less serene fashion
  Still we look: around our margin
    Holy priestess, longing lover,
  Poet musing, vagrant virgin,
    Nor their own mild looks discover,
But the light and glow of that they are meditating over.

ORPHEUS.

    O curves unbeholden,
      Bright glory of bays!
    Deep gulfs grown golden
      With dawn and its ways!
    With sunset enfolden
      In silvery praise!
Come forth! I invoke ye, O gulfs, where the sea is a children, and plays.

Aleister Crowley

THE BAYS.

Where the hills reach to heaven behind us
  A voice is rolled over the steep,
Some godhead whose glory would bind us,
  Reflected far-off on the deep.
We hear the low chant that may blind us,
  The song from the ultimate shore.
We come that our lover may find us
  His bride as he found us before.
We listen, and love; and his voice is the voice of the God we adore.

ORPHEUS.

  Come forth in your gladness,
    O end of all these!
  O sorrow and madness
    And passion and ease,
  Sharp joy and sweet sadness,
    Deep life and deep peace!
Come forth! I invoke you, ringed round earth's girdle, the manifold seas!

THE SEA.

I hear but one voice in our voices;
  One tune, multitudinous notes;
One life that burns low or rejoices,
  One song from the numberless throats.
Where ice on my bosom is piled,
  Where palm-fronded islands begem
My breast, where I rage in the wild
  White storms, where I lap the low hem
Of earth's mantle, or war on her crags, I am one, and my soul is in them.

  I am mother of earth and her daughter;
    I am father of heaven and his son;
  I am fire in the palace of water;
    I am God, and my glory is one!
  I am bride of the sun and the starlight;
    The moonlight is bride unto me;
  I am lit of my deeps with a far light,
    My heart and its flame flung free.
I am She, the beginning and end; I am all, and my name is the Sea!

ORPHEUS.

  Then thou, O my mother,
    Hast given to me
  The power of another,
    The watery key.
  Bright air is my brother,
    My sister the sea;
I have called, and they answer and come; and their song is but glory to thee.

Orpheus

    One other is left me,
      The light of the earth.
    If Fate had bereft me,
      Oh Muse, of thy birth,
    Still I had cleft me
      A way in her girth!
I tune the loud lyre once again to the mother of men in her mirth.

    O mighty and glad
      In spring-time and summer!
    O tearful and sad
      When the sun is grown dumber,
    When the season is mad,
      And the gods overcome her,
When the sky is fulfilled of the frost and the fingers of winter numb her!

    O marvellous earth
      Of multiple mood
    That givest men birth
      And delicate food,
    Red wine to make mirth
      Of thine own red blood.
And corn and green grass and sweet flowers and fruits most heavenly-hued!

    Borne skyward in swoon
      By arrowy hours,
    Girt round of the moon
      And the girdling flowers,
    The sun for a boon,
      Sweet kisses of showers,
O mother, O life, O desire, my soul is a bird in thy bowers!

    My soul is caught up
      In thy green-hearted waves.
    I drink at the cup
      Of thy sweet valley graves.
    My spirit may sup
      Slow tunes in thy caves.
O hide me, thy child, in thy bosom, that the heart in me yearns to and craves.

    Most virginally sprung
      In the shadow of light,
    Eternally young,
      A magical sight,
    Wandering among
      Day, twilight, and night,
As a bride in her chamber that dreams many visions of varied delight.

    O how shall my lyre
      Divide thee, dispart
    Thy water and fire,
      Thy soul and thy heart,
    Thy hills that spring higher,

Aleister Crowley

Thy flowers that upstart,
How quire thee, my limitless love, with a lewd and a limited art?

  A fortress, a sphere,
   An arrow of flame;
  Let thy children appear
   At the sound of thy name!
  In my silence uprear
   The sweet guerdon of shame!
Be they choral to hymn thee, O mother, thy magic ineffable fame!

  Last birth of the Sun,
   Best gift of the giver,
  Thou surely art One!
   As the moon on the river,
  Whose star-blossoms run,
   Kiss, tremble, and shiver,
And roll into ultimate space, and are lost to man's vision for ever.

  Come forth to the sound
   Of the lightning lyre,
  Ye valleys profound
   As a man's desire,
  Ye woodlands bound
   In the hills that are higher
Than even the note of a bird as it wings to the solar fire!

  Ye fruits and corn,
   Gold, rose, and green,
  Vines purple-born,
   Pearl-hidden sheen,
  Trees waving in scorn
   Of the grass between!
Come forth in your chorus, and chant the praise of your mother and queen!

  Ye trees many-fronded
   That shake to the wind,
  Green leaves that have sounded
   My harp in our kind,
  Light boughs that are rounded,
   Grey tops that are shrined
In the tears of the heaven as they fall in the blackening storm grown blind!

  Ye fields that are flowered
   In purple and white,
  Embossed and embowered
   By the love of the light,
  Gold-sandalled and showered,
   Dew-kissed of the night,
Your song is too faint and too joyous for mortals to hear it aright.

  Blue pansies, and roses,
   And poppies of red,

Orpheus

    Pale violets in posies
      Where Hyacinth bled,
    The flower that closes
      Its dolorous head; --
What song may be sung, or what tune may be told, or what word may be said?

    All tropical scent,
      Blossom-kindled perfume
    Love-colours new-lent
      By the infinite womb,
    Gold subtlety blent
      Wit the scarlet bloom; --
Shall ye in my melody live? Shall my song be not rather your tomb?

    Most musical moves
      The head of the corn;
    Strong glorious loves
      Of its being are born.
    Dim shadows of groves
      Of Demeter adorn
The waves and the woods of the earth, the heart of the mother forlorn.

    Caves curved of the wind,
      Deep hollows of earth,
    Whence the song of the blind
      Old prophet had birth,
    The caves that confined
      Deep music of mirth,
Thy caves, O my mother, are these not a gem in thy virginal girth?

    Ye mountains uplift
      As an arrow in air;
    Ice-crowned, rock-cliffed,
      Snow-bosomed bare,
    I give ye the gift
      Of a voice more fair.
Leave echo, and wake, and proclaim that ye stand against death and despair!

    Ye hills where I rested
      In rapture of life,
    From dawn calm-breasted
      To evening's strife,
    Where skies were nested
      With mist for a wife!
Leave echo, and speak for yourselves; let your song pierce the heaven as a knife!

    Olympus alone
      Of earth's glories is taken
    For deity's throne
      deep-frozen, storm-shaken.
    What glories are shown
      When their slumbers awaken!
The avalanche thunders adown, and the gods of the gods are forsaken.

To mortals your voices
   Are mighty and glad.
The maiden rejoices:
   The man is grown mad
For love, and his choice is
   The choice of a lad
When a virgin first smiles on his suit, and the summer for envy is sad.

Wan grows Aphrodite,
   And Artemis frail;
Apollo less mighty,
   Red Bacchus too pale.
Dark Hades grows bright he
   Alone may avail
When the god and the moral are one, as the mountain is one with the gale.

THE CHILDREN OF EARTH.

Our hair deep laden with the scent of earth,
The colour of her rosy body's birth,
   Our mother, lady and life of all that is divine;
We gather to the sombre sound, as spring
Had whispered, "Follow," hiding in her wing
   Her glorious head and flowing breast of wine.
Though in the hollow of her heart be set
So deep and awful a fire, though the net
   Of all her robes be frail as we are fine,
We gather, listening to the living lyre
Like falling water shot with amber fire,
And blown aloft by winds even to heaven's desire.

Deep starry gems set in a silver sea,
Sullen low voices of dark minstrelsy,
   Light whispers of strange loves, of silver woven,
Dumb kisses and wild laughter following:
All these as lives of autumn and of spring
   We are: we follow across the rainbow cloven,
A never-fading path of golden glory,
Whereof the lone Leucadian promontory
   Holds one divinest gate: the other troven
Far, far beyond in interlunar skies,
Where the Himalayas stir them, and arise
To listen to the song that swells our arteries.

O moving labyrinth sun-crowned, dread maze
Of starry paths, of Zeus-untrodden ways,
   Of mystic vales unfooted of the deep,
Our mother, virgin yet in many places
Unseen of man, beholden of the faces
   Only of elemental shapes of sleep
That are ourselves, her daughters wild and fair

Orpheus

Caught nymphwise in the kisses of the air,
That flings our songs reverberate from steep to steep,
Songs caught in solar light, we are shed
Even down beyond the valleys of the dead,
And smiled upon in groves ruled by the holy head.

Great Pan hath heard us, children of his wooing,
Great Pan, that listens to the forest, suing
  Vainly His peace that dwells even in the desolate halls.
The delicately-chiselled flowers nod,
Look to the skies, and see thee for a God,
  O sightless lyre that wails, O viewless voice that calls!
Thy sound is in our death and in her womb,
Far in Spring's milky breast, in Autumn's gloom,
  In Summer's feast and song, in Winter's funerals.
In the dead hollow of the hills there rings,
Sharp song, like frost hissing on silver wings,
Or like the swelling tune we listen to for Spring's.

We come, we mountains, crowned and incense-bringing,
Robed as white priests, the solemn anthem singing;
  Or as an organ thundering fiery tunes.
We come, we greener hills, and rend the sky,
With happier chorus and the songs that die
  Or mix their subtle joy and being with the moon's.
We come, we pine-clad steeps, we feathery slopes,
With footfalls softer than the antelope's.
  We listen and obey: the sacred slumberer swoons
More tranced than death in this far following,
Careless of winter, not invoking spring;
And all the witless woods company us and sing.

But not the glades by song of thee unstricken?
Not they? Shall they refuse the pulse to quicken,
  Soft smiting the low melody of light?
Tuned without fingers, the wild woods lift high
The wordless chant, the murmurous melody,
  The song that dwells like moon-inkindled night.
We draw from low palm groves and cedar hills,
From stern grey slumbers, for thy music fills
  All earth with unimaginable delight.
Have we not brought the leaves dew-diamonded,
The buds fresh-gleaming, star-blossoms, and shed
Our scent and colour and song around thy sacred head?

We that are flowers are kindled in thy praise,
Even as thy song shed lustre and swift rays,
  Darting to brighten and open the folded flowers.
The violet lifts its head, the lily lightens,
The daisy shakes its dew, the pansy brightens,
  All cups of molten light upon the twilight hours.
The poppy flames anew, the buttercup
Glows with fresh fire, the larkspur rouses up

Aleister Crowley

To be the lark indeed amid the azalea bowers.
Magnolia and light blooms of roses mute
Rouse them to gather in one golden lute
In fairy light and song into the sky to shoot.

The laughing companies of corn awaken,
Their wind-swept waves by Dædal music taken
   Into a golden heaven of festal song.
We shake and glisten in the sun, we see
The very soul and majesty of thee
   Thrill in the lyre and leave the lazy long
Notes for crisp magic of sharp rustling sound,
And thy life quickens and thy loves abound,
   Listening the answer of our dancing throng.
Joy, sleep, peace, laughter, thought, remembrance, came
Even at our prelude, a death-quickening flame,
And earth rejoiced throughout to hear Demeter's name.

We come, in bass deep-swelling, rocks and caves,
A hollow roar across the golden waves
   Hidden in islands set deep in the untravelled sea.
Across the corn from storm-cleft mountainsides
Our voice peals, like the thunder of the tides,
   Into the darkling hills that fringe Eternity.
Dire and divine our womb unfruitful bears
Deep music darker than tempestuous airs.
   When Heaven's anger wakes: when at our own decree,
With clanging rocks sky-piercing for our tomb,
We call the thunder from our own black womb,
We hear the voice and we obey -- we know not whom!

We hear thee, who are cliffs and pinnacles
Higher than heaven's base, founded far in hell's;
   We hear, that sunder the blue skies of heaven;
Our voiceless clefts and spires of delicate hue,
Changing and lost in the exultant blue,
   By fire and whirlwind fashioned and then riven,
Invoke fresh song, with deep solemnity
In noble notes of mastery answering thee,
   By some young tumult in our old hearts driven;
And this immortal path of splintered rock
Shall lead the wild chant to the sky, and mock
The nectared feast of Gods with its impassioned shock.

Deep-mouthed, I, earthquake, wake in echoing thunder.
I break my mother's breast; I rear asunder
   The womb that bore me; I arise in terror,
Threatening to ruin her, crag, crown, and column,
Reverberate music of that mighty and solemn
   Call of creation, Vulcan's awful mirror.
I rend the sky with clamour terrible,
Shaking the thrones of earth and heaven and hell,
   Confound the universe in universal error.

Orpheus

I sound the awful note that summons mortals,
As I awake, to pass the dreadful portals
And face the gloom of Dis, the unnameable immortals.

Soft our mild music steals through thunderous pauses,
A phrase made magic by the Second Causes,
  The mighty Ones that dwell beneath the empyrean.
We, vines and fruits and trees with autumn laden,
Sing as the bride-song of a married maiden
  Before the god-like vigour of the man
Breaks the frail temple-doors of love asunder,
And wakes the new life's promise in pale wonder,
  Shattering the moulded glass, the shape Selenian.
Fruits of the earth, our low song joins the crowd.
We need not (to be heard) to thunder loud.
Our hearts are lifted up, our heads with love low bowed.

The tenderest light, the deepest hidden, is shed
Up through dark earth -- your home, O happy dead! --
  Crusted in darkness lie the secret lights.
Formed in the agony of earth as tears,
Clothed in the crystal mirror of the years,
  We dwell, sweet-hearted nun-like eremites!
Diamond and ruby, topaz and sapphire,
Emerald and amethyst, one clear bright fire,
  We are earth's stars below, as she above hath Night's.
Our sweet clean song pierces the cover,
And thin keen notes of music flit and hover
Like spirit-birds upon the lyre of this our lover.

We, children of the mountains, lying low
On earth's own bosom, deep, embowered, flow
  In wide soft waves of land: upon us sweep
The mightiest rivers: in our hollows lie
Great lakes: our voices hardly rise, but die
  In the cold streams of air: shallow and deep:
Leagues by the thousand, dells a minute long;
All we are children of the mighty throng
  That cluster where the mountains fail, and sleep
In such cool peace that even the lyre awakes
Hardly a soul that tenderer music makes.
Yet we arise and listen for our own sweet sakes.

THE LIVING CREATURES OF THE EARTH.

  The heavy hand is held,
    And the whips leave weary blows.
  The mysteries of eld
    Are cancelled and expelled,
    And the miserable throes.

  All we are shapen fair

Aleister Crowley

In many forms of grace,
But change is everywhere,
And time is all our share
  And all the ways of space.

One lives an hour of day;
  One even man's life exceeds;
One loves to chase and slay;
One loves to sing and play;
  Each soul to his own deeds!

A share of joy is ours,
  A double share of grief;
So sum the many hours
In many hopes and powers,
  All powers except the chief.

Emotion fills our souls,
  And love delights us well,
And joy of sense full rolls;
But leads us, and controls
  Life's central citadel.

Whence we were drawn who knows?
  Of law or Gods or chance?
But, as life's river flows,
What Sea shall clasp and close
  Beyond blind circumstance?

Such little power we own
  Of vague experience,
And instinct to enthrone
The life's mere needs alone,
  Nor answer "why" and "whence."

Nor wandering in the night
  Our minds may apprehend
Reflecting in pure light
Of soul, what sound or sight
  May lead us to some end.

We hear the dim sound roll
  From distant mountains drawn,
We follow, but no soul
Guesses that silver goal,
  The sunset or the dawn.

The lyre entices fast
  Our willing feet and wings,
We wonder from the past
What spell is overcast
  From of the sonant strings.

Orpheus

Awhile we deem our mates
  Are calling through the wood;
Awhile the tune creates
These unfamiliar states
  Of thinking solitude.

Awhile we gather clear
  A note of promise swell,
A song of fate and fear,
Assuring us who hear
  Of other shapes to dwell.

A promise vast and grand
  As is the spangled sky!
We dimly understand;
We join the following band
  Of dancing greenery!

We see all nature bend
  To high Olympus' hill.
Our tunes we choose and send;
We follow to the end,
  O Orpheus, all thy will.

Our little love and hate,
  Our hunger and our fear,
Pass to a solemn state
Pregnant with hope and fate.
  O Orpheus, we are here!

THE EARTH.

Life hidden in death,
  Life shrined in the soul,
Life bright for his breath,
  Life dark for his goal,
I am Mother, and Burier, and Friend --
Look thou to the end!

I am Light in thy Love,
  I am Love in thy Life.
I am cloistered above
  Where the stars are at strife.
I am life in thy light, and thy death
Is part of my breath.

My voices are many,
  Thy lyre is but one;
But thou art not as any
  Soul under the sun!
Thou hast power for an hour,
The motherly dower.

One voice of my voices
  Uncalled and unheard,
No song that rejoices
  Of beast or of bird,
No sound of my children sublime,
  But the spirit of time.

Fear is his name,
  Nor flickers nor dies
His blackening flame.
  Beware, were thou wise!
Not him shalt thou hail from the dusk with thy breath;
  His name -- it is Death!

My seasons and years,
  Shalt thou traffic with these?
Art thou Fate? Are her shears
  Asleep or at ease?
Though Time were no more than the shape of thy glass --
  Beware! let him pass!

ORPHEUS.

Not these do I fear,
  O Earth, for their peace.
I cry till they hear
  O'er the desolate seas.
I call ye! give ear,
  O seasons, to these
Fleet-footed, the strings of the lyre! Come forth! I invoke ye – and cease.

O hours of the day,
  And hours of the night,
Pause now while ye may
  In your heavenly flight!
Give answer and say,
  Have I called ye aright?
Are the strings of my lyre as fire, the voice of my singing as light?

THE HOURS.

Darkness and daylight in divided measure
  Gather as petals of the sunflower,
In many seasons seek the lotus-treasure,
Following as dancing maidens, mute for pleasure,
  The fervent flying footsteps of the Hour.

The sun looks over the memorial hills,
  The trampling of his horse heard as wind;
He leaps and turns, and all his fragrance fills
The shade and silence; all the rocks and rills
  Ring with the triumph of his steeds behind.

Orpheus

The bright air winnowed by the plumeless leapers
  Laughs, and the low light pierces to the bed
Where lovers linger, where the smiling sleepers
Stir, and the herds unmindful of their keepers
  Low for pure love of morning's dewy head.

The morning shakes its ocean-bathed tresses,
  The bright sun broadens over all the earth.
The green leaves fall, fall into his caresses,
And all the world's heart leaps, again addresses
  Its life, and girds it in the golden girth.

Then noon full-fashioned lies upon the steep.
  The large sun sighs and turns his bridle-rein,
Thinks of the ocean, turns his heart to sleep,
Laughing no longer, not yet prone to weep,
  Feeling the prelude of the coming pain.

The hills and dales are dumb beneath the heat,
  And all the world lies tranced or mutely dreaming,
Save some low sigh caught up where pulses beat
Of warm love waiting in the arboreal seat
  Till the shade lengthen on the lawn light-gleaming.

Now all the birds change tune, and all the light
  Glows lowlier, musing on departed day.
Strange wings and sombre, heralding the night,
Fleet far across the woods; and gleaming bright
  The evening star looks from the orient way.

Shadow and silence deepen: all the woods
  Take on a tenderer phrase of musical
Breezes: the stream-sought homes and solitudes
Murmur a little where the maiden moods
  Are sadder as the evening's kisses fall.

Like silver scales of serpenthood they fall
  Across the blind air of the evening;
Shadowy ghosts arise funereal
And seek unspeakable things; and dryads call
  The satyr-company to the satyr-king.

And all the light is over; but the sky
  Shudders with blanched light of the unrisen moon.
The night-birds mingle their sad minstrelsy
For daylight's requiem: and the sea's reply
  Now stirs across the land's departed tune.

The moon is up: the choral crowd of stars,
  Shapen like strange or unknown animals,
Move in their measure: beyond Æolian bars
The clustering winds, moving as nenuphars,
  Gather and muse before the midnight calls.

The darkness is most deep in hollow dells.
  There, blacker than Cocytus, lurk the shades
Darker than death's, more terrible than hell's,
Uttering unwritten words: the silent wells
  Keep their sweet secret till the morning maids

Bring their carved pitchers to the moss-grown side.
  For now beyond, below the east, appears
A hint as if a band, silvern and wide,
The girdle of some goddess amber-eyed,
  Rose from the solemn company of the spheres.

The sky is tinged, as if the amorous flesh
  Of that same queen shown through the girdle drawn
By here own kissing fervour through its mesh.
Last, glory of godhead! flickers, flames the fresh
  First faint frail rose and arrow of the dawn.

SPRING.

Mild glimpses of the quiet moon, let through
  Tall groves of ceder, stain the glade; gleams mild
The kirtle of the unweaned spring, stained blue
  From the blue breasts that suckle to the child.
    Through the new-leaved trees
    The hidden stranger sees
The moon's sweet light, the shadows listening
    If a ghost-foot should fall:
    And if a ghost voice call
Tremble the leaves and light-streaks of the spring.
On wavering wing
  The small clouds gallop in the windy sky:
    The hoarse rooks croak and droop them to the nest:
One sweet small throat begins to sing,
  Becomes the song, losing identity
    Ere its wail wakes the long low-lying crest
    That rears across the west.

Spring, maiden-footed, steals across the space,
  Sandalled with tremulous light, with flickering hair
Blown o'er the sweet looks of the fair child-face,
  Like willows drooping o'er the liquid mere,
    Whence timid eyes look far,
    Even where her kisses are
Awaited by the tender mother lips,
    Earth's, that is lonely and old,
    Grown sad, fearful, and cold
With bitter winter and the sun's eclipse;
So the child slips
  From bough to bough between the weeping trees,
    And with frail fingers smooths and touches them.
They murmur in their sleep: the moonlight dips

Orpheus

And laughs, seeing how young buds catch life from these
Child-kisses on the stem.

The leaves laugh low, and frosty-footed Time
  Shoulders a lighter burden; in the dale
Some distant notes of lovely music climb,
    Thrown from the golden-throated nightingale,
    Pale sobs of love and life
    With death and fear at strife,
Fiercely beset and hardly conquering,
    When spring's bright eyes at last
    Flash through the sullen past,
And tune its pain to tears, its peace to sing.
The earth's lips cling
  To the child's bosom, and low smiles revive;
  Love is new-born upon the golden hour,
And all the life of all the exultant spring
  Breathes in the wind that wakes the world alive
    Into the likeness of a flower.

SUMMER.

Full is the joy of Maidenhood made strong,
  Too proud to bend to swift Apollo's kiss;
Rejoicing in its splendour, and the throng
  Of gaunt hounds leashless before Artemis.
  In strange exulting bliss
The maiden stands, full-grown, with bounding breasts
  Bared to the noon, and narrow
Keen eyes that glance, dim fires that veil their crests
  To flame along the arrow
Aimed at some gallant of ten tines perched high
Branching against the sky
  His cedar-spreading horns: erect she stands,
  Holding in glimmering hands
    A silver bow across the shining weather,
  While, bound in pearl-wrought bands,
    Her bright hair streams; she draws the quivering feather
Back to the small ear curved: with golden zone
  Gathering her limbs she stands alone
    Like a young antelope poised upon a spire of stone.

What tender lightning flashes in the bosom
  Heaving with vigour of young life? What storm
Gathers across the brow's broad lotus-blossom?
  What sudden passion fills the fragrant form
  With subtle streams of warm
Blood tingling to the finger-tips of rose?
    Swiftly the maiden closes
The lustre of her look: disdainful glows
    The fire of wreathing roses
In her bright cheeks: she darts away to find
Like some uncovered hind

Shade in the forest from the stag's pursuit,
Ere the sun's passion shoot
His ray, strange deeps unknown and feared to uncover.
 But now the ancient root
Of some wise oak betrays her to her lover:
 She stumbles and falls prone: the forest noon
 Guesses life's law; all nature's tune
 Tell that the hour is come when May must grow to June.

Then in the broad glare of the careless sun
 Apollo's light is on her and within;
His shafts of glory pierce her one by one;
 His kisses darken, shivering and keen,
 Swift glories cold and clean
Of that chaste bridal, and the earth gets gladness,
 Till the last winter's traces
Fall from the spring's last cold wind -- shining sadness! --
 And from the frail new faces
Blushing through moss; and all the world is light
With the unsufferably bright
 Full joy and guerdon of that sunny season
 By Love's sweet trap of treason.
 So the bright girl is now a woman brighter;
 And childhood sees a reason
 Beneath the strong stroke of the goodly smiter
For all the past: and love at last is hers.
No more the bosom's pride demurs,
While in her womb the first faint pulse of motherhood soft stirs.

AUTUMN.

Full amber-breasted light of harvest-moon,
 And sheaves of corn remembering the sun
 Laughing again for love of that caress
When night is fallen, and the sleepy swoon
 Of warm waves lap the shoreland, one by one;
 Forgetful kisses like a dream's possess
All the low-lying land,
 And, statelier than the swaying form
 Of some loud God, lifting the storm
In his disastrous hand,
 Steps the sweet-voiced, the mellow motherhood
 Glad of the sun's kiss, full of life, well wooed
 And won and brought to his bed,
Proud of her rhythm in the lusty kiss,
 Triumphant and exulting in the mood
Wherein her being is
 Crowned with a husband's head,
 And left in solitude which is not solitude.

She strides with mighty steps across the glade
 Laughing, her bosom swelling with the milk
 Born of a million kisses: leaps her womb

Orpheus

Pregnant with fruits, and latter flowers, and shade
Of the great cedar-groves: soft, soft, as silk,
  Her skin glows amber, silvered with the bloom
Mist-like of the moon's light,
  A slumberous haze of quietude
  Shed o'er the hardy limbs, and lustihood,
And boldness, and great might.
Earth knows her daring daughter, and the sea
Breaks into million-folded mystery
  Of flower-like flashes in the pale moon-rise,
Exulting also, now the sun is faded,
  With joy of her supreme fertility
And glowing masteries
  Of autumn summer-shaded,
  The golden fruit of all the blossoming sky.

And now the watcher to the bright breasts blind
  Loses the seemly shape, the loud swift song;
  Now the moon falls, and all the gold is gone,
And round the storm-caught shape hard gusts of wind
  Blow, and her leaves are torn, a flying throng
  Of orange and purple and red; the sombre sun
Shines darkly in her breast
  But wakes no joy therein,
  And all his kisses sharp and keen
Bring only now desire of rest,
  Not their old rapture: the warm violet eyes
  Melt into sweet hot tears; subtler the sighs
    Are interfused with death;
The brave bright looks grow duller,
  And fear is mingled with love's ecstasies
Again, and all her breath
    Fails, and the shape and colour
    Fade, fail, are lost in the sepulchral seas.

WINTER.

Know ye my children? From the old strong breast
  Not weary yet of life's grey change, not drawn
  Into the utter peace of death, the rest
  Of the dim hour that lingers ere the dawn,
Spring these that laugh upon thee. In the snow
    See forest bare and gaunt,
    Where winged whispers haunt,
Lighting the dull sky with a slumberous glow;
  Hear the strange sounds of winter chaunt;
Feel the keen wisdom of the winter thrill
  Young hearts with passionate foretaste
    Of death in some wild waste
Of deserts darkening at some wild god's will,
Of frozen steeps awaiting the repose
  That only death discovers, never sleep.
    My misery is this

That I must wake to childhood gold and rose,
  And maidenhood, and wifehood, and still keep
    Bound on Life's fatal wheel -- revolving bliss.

O that worn wisdom and the age of sorrow
  Could learn its bitter lesson, and depart
Into some nightfall guiltless of a morrow,
  Into some cave's unprofitable heart
Beyond this curse of birth! O that dread night
  Could come and cover all,
    Even itself to fall
To some abyss past resurrection's might!
  For the old whispers of my old life call
  Accursed hopes, accursed fears, accursed pleasures.
    Long-suffering of all life!
    Changed consciousness at strife!
No dancer treads the melancholy measures
Unchanged for one short tune: no dancer flags,
  The hateful music luring them to move
    Weary and desolate;
And as the rhyme revolves and shrills and drags
  Their limbs insane they smile and call it love,
    Or, mocking, call it hatred: it is Fate.

These grey eyes close to the deceitful dream
  Of death that will not take the tired for ever.
Again, again, revolves the orb; the stream,
  The dew, the cloud, the ocean, and the river.
My magic wand and cup and sword and spell
    Languish, forgotten fears.
    The cup is filled with tears;
The sword is red with blood; the pentacle
    Builded of flesh; the wand its snake-head rears
Swift energy: my labour is but lost.
  I, who thus thought all things to end,
    Find in the void no friend.
I have but conjured up the fiend that most
I trusted to abolish: all my toil
  Goes to give rest to life, and build anew
    These pinnacles of pain,
Cupola upon cupola; the soil
  To comfort, to avail, to assoil with dew,
    To build the year again.

ORPHEUS.

    O hours not of day
      But of æons that roll!
    Earth stretches away
      From pole unto pole;
    Four season decay,
      Ere one sound of thy soul,
O fervent and following years, springs over the solar goal!

Orpheus

    Come forth to the sound
      Of the seven sweet strings!
    Advance and rebound!
      Be your pomp as a king's!
    Girdled around
      With season and stings
As a serpent's encompassing Time. Come forth! on the heavy grey wings!

    Ye arbiter lords
      That sit as for doom,
    Bright splendour of swords
      Leaps forth in your gloom!
    But stronger my chords
      Shall lift in your womb
The love of your passage and time, immemorial ages, your tomb.

    Ye linger for long,
      But ye pass and are done:
    But I, my sweet song
      Outliveth the sun!
    Ye are many and strong;
      I am stronger, and one!
Come forth! I invoke ye, O years, in my evening orison.

THE YEARS.

Crowned with Eternity, beyond beginning;
  Sandalled with wings, Eternity's; the end
Far beyond sight of striving soul or sinning;
  Ourselves see not, nor know, nor comprehend.
Reeling from chaos, unto Chronos winning,
  Devoured of Him our Father and our friend,
This is our life, lead winged or footed golden;
We pass, and each of other is unbeholden.

Ranged in dim spectral order and procession,
  We span man's thought, we limit him in time;
None of the souls of earth have had possession
  Of larger lovers or passions more sublime.
Where the night-caverns hide our solemn session
  The summoning word lifts up our holy rhyme.
Even as a mighty river, bend to bend,
We rise in turn and look toward the end.

Also, the Gods arisen from the living
  Lights of the sky, half hidden in the night,
Vast shapes beholden of men unbelieving,
  Staggering the sense and reason with the sight,
Manifold, mighty, monstrous, no light giving
  Unto the soul that is not also light; --
We rise in ghastly power; we know the token,
The speech of silence and the song unspoken.

ORPHEUS.

Come forth to the sound.
  Ye lustres of years
  Hide in profound
  Abysses of fears.
  Hidden and bound!
  The voice of tears
Implores and impels ye, O lustres, with a tune that is strong as a seer's.

THE LUSTRES.

Fivefold the shape sublime that lifts its head
  Uniform, self-repeating, comparable
At last to a man's life: twice seven times dead
  Ere the light flickers in that citadel,
Or the great whiteness lure his soul instead
  Of many-coloured earth: ere the strong spell
Fail, and the Fates with iron-shapen shears
Cut the frail silver, hide him from the years.

Fivefold: the year that is in darkness hidden,
  Being beginning: then the moving year,
All change and tumult; then the quiet unchidden
  Of deep reflection; then the gladdening tear
Or saddening smile, the laughter not forbidden
  And love enfolding the green-woven sphere:
Lastly, the burning year of flame and fume
That burns me up in fire's sepulchral womb.

Fivefold: the child, the frail, the delicate:
  Then the strong laughing mischief: then the proud
Fight toward manhood and the sense elate,
  Creative power and passion: then the loud
Assertion of young will, the quickening rate
  And strength in blood, in youth with life endowed,
And firmness fastening; the last lustre's span
Consolidates and shows the perfect man.

Fivefold: the humour changes as his child
  Calls him first "father"; a sense of strength divine
Fills him; then man's work in the world, and wild
  Efforts to fame: then steadier in the shrine
Burns the full flame: then, turning, the years piled
  Seem suddenly a burden; then the fine
Flavour of full maturity is tasted:
The man looks back, and asks if life be wasted.

Fivefold: delight in woman altering
  To joy of sunlight only: love of life
Changing to fear of death: the golden spring
  Trembles; he hates the cold, the winter strife,

Orpheus

Laughs not with lust of combat: feebly cling
 His old hands: he has sepultured his wife:
Last, palsied, shaking, drawing tremorous breath,
He gasps -- and stumbles in the pit of death.

ORPHEUS.

 O girded and spanned
  By the deeds of time,
 Rocks shattered and planned
  In your depth: where climb
 The race and the land,
  And the growth sublime
Of worlds -- I invoke ye! Come forth, ye centuries! Come to the rhyme!

THE CENTURIES.

How hardly a man
 Though his strength were as spring's
Shall stretch out his span
 To the width of my wings!
The years are enfolden
In my bosom golden,
My periods
Are the hours of the Gods.
They have their plan
 In my seasons; all things
Are woven in the span
 Of the spread of my wings.

My brazen gates cleft
 By shafts shed of time,
Are ruined and left
 As the Gods sing their rhyme.
Buttress and joist are
Effaced of the cloister.
Fane after fane
We lift us again
To the hoarier transept
 Where ages climb,
And ruin is left
 Where the Gods said their rhyme.

The deity-year
 (Whereof I am an hour)
Shall be born and appear
 As the birth of a flower,
Shall fade as they faded,
The flower wreaths braided
In maiden's hair.
The Gods shall fare
As the children of Fear
 In the Fear-God's Power,

And their names disappear
  As the fall of a flower!

The universe-day
  (Whereof I am a second)
Shall fall away
  And be no more reckoned;
Shall fall into ruin.
(Sad garden it grew in!)
Unguessed at, unknown,
Beyond them alone,
Is a space that is grey
  As it caught them, and beckoned,
And lost them -- their way
  Is not counted nor reckoned!

Inconceivable hollow,
  Eternity's womb!
Cataclysmal they follow,
  Tomb hidden in tomb.
Reeled off and unspun,
Time's fashion is done
In the ultimate
Abysses of fate.
Æons they swallow,
  And swamp in the gloom,
Where Eternities follow
  Their biers to their tomb.

ORPHEUS.

O Mother, O hollow
  Sweet heart of the moon!
O matchless Apollo
  That granted the tune!
Time's children follow
  The strings that commune
With Nature well cloven that comes to the lyre's lilt silver hewn.

O bays of the wind,
  And shoreland of Thrace!
O beaten and blind
  In the light of my face!
Heaven thunders behind,
  Hell shakes for a space,
As I fling the loud sound to the sky, and the vaults of the Earth give place.

O mystical tune
  Of a magic litten
Of music, the moon,
  The stars unsmitten,
The sun, the unhewn
  Stones deeply bitten

Orpheus

By runic fingers of time, where decrees of the Fates are written!

    Time listens, obeys me;
      All Nature replies;
    Nought avoids me, nor stays me,
      Nor checks, nor defies.
    Tribute she pays me
      From seas unto skies.
But Death -- shall he heed me or hear? shall he list to the lyre and arise?

    O thou who art seated,
      Invisible king,
    The never-defeated,
      The shadowy thing!
    What mortal hath greeted
      Thy shrine, but shall sing
Not earthly but tunes of thine own, in the vaults of Aornos that ring?

    Nor caring nor hearing
      For hearts that be bowed,
    Nor hating nor fearing
      Man's crying aloud,
    Solemnly spearing
      The single, the crowd,
Thou sittest remote and alone, unprofane, with due silence endowed!

    I call thee by Nature,
      My mother and friend!
    By every creature!
      By life and its end!
    By love, the true teacher,
      My chanting I send,
Invoking thy stature immense, the terrible form of a fiend!

    I hear not a word,
      Though my music be rolled
    As the song of a bird
      Through fields of gold.
    Hast thou not heard?
      Have I not told
The magic that bridleth the Gods, the Gods in their houses of old?

    Art thou elder than they
      In their mountain of light?
    Is thy fugitive way
      Lost in uttermost night?
    Shalt thou not obey,
      Or my lyre not affright,
If I call thee by Heaven and Earth with a God's tumultuous might?

    If I curse thee or chide
      Shalt thou tremble not, Thou?
    Not move thee and hide

From the light of my brow?
Shall my arrows divide
Not the heart of thee now?
Art thou cased in strong iron to mock the spells that all others avow?

    Art thou muffled or hidden
      In adamant brass?
    Is my music forbidden
      In Orcus to pass?
    Have I cursed thee and chidden?
      My flesh being grass,
I curse not as yet, but command thee; the names that avail I amass.

    No sound? no whisper?
      No answer to me?
    From dawn-star to Hesper
      I call upon thee!
    In the hour of vesper
      I change the key!
I cry on Apollo to aid, I lift up my lyre on the sea.

    Thou reaper of fear,
      Accurst of mankind,
    I charge thee to hear,
      Deaf horror deep-mined
    In hell! O uprear
      On the front of the wind!
I curse thee! Thou hearest my hounds of thunder that mutter behind?

    How strange is the dark
      And the silence around!
    Hardly the spark
      Of my silvery sound
    Moves, or may mark
      The heaven's dim bound.
How strange! I have sought him in vain -- perchance not in vain have I found!

    No! Life thrills in me;
      Vibrates on lyre;
    The Fates still spin me
      Their thread of desire:
    Still, woo and win me
      Soft eyes, and the dire
Low fervour of sensual phrase, song kin to the nethermost fire!

    In silence I wait
      For his voice to roll,
    For the coming of Fate,
      The strength of my soul.
    My words create
      One glorious whole
From the fragments divided that seem past a man's or a god's control

Orpheus

    I, seeing the life
      Of the flowers renew,
    The victorious strife
      Of the spring run through,
    The child's birth rife
      With loftier dew --
I know the deep truth in myself; see acacia in cypress and yew.

    Death is not at all!
      'Tis a mask or a dream!
    The things that befall
      Only slumber or seem!
    They fear; they appal --
      They are not as ye deem!
Death died when I dipped my lure in the sweet Heliconian stream!

    Give praise to your lord,
      All souls that draw breath,
    All flowers of the sward!
      For the song of me saith:
    "Sound the loud chord!
      Let love be a wreath!
Death is not for ye any more, for I am the Master of Death!"

PARABASIS.

    As I sit in the sound
      Of the wash of the surf,
    On the long low ground,
      The trees and the turf;
    In front the profound,
      The warrior seas,
      Upstirred of the breeze,
    By the far reed bound --
I know the low music of love, I feel the sweet murmur in me,
      My soul is in tune with the sea.

    The stars are above me,
    The rocks are below me,
      The sea is around!
    Great Gods that love me
    Lead me, and show me.
      Their powers profound.
    Their lightnings move me
    To stir me, to throw me
      As into a swound,
The song of the infinite surf that is beaten and bound
      As a fierce wolf-hound,
The song that lures me, and lifts men, and mingles my soul into sound!

    O Nature, my mother,
      Heart melted on heart
    At last! Not another,

Aleister Crowley

    Not any shall part
      Thy soul from my art.
    How should it be otherwise,
      Sister divine,
    Lover, my mother wise,
      Wiser than wine?
    Seeing I linger
      Here on the beach --
    Let God's own finger
      Here to me reach,
    Making me singer
      Each unto each --
    Nature and Man made one
    In the light and fire of the sun,
      And the sobbing tune
      Of the moon,
    Wedded in cyclic bonds,
    Where fall the aeon-fronds,
      Whose large bed bears a child
        (In its due period)
    Not merciful and not severe,
    Knowing nor love nor fear,
      But majesty most mild,
        Being indeed a God.

Yea, let the very ray-hand of Apollo
Lead me where none may follow
Save in blind eagle-fury and full flight
Pythian against the light,
Writing in all the sea, the trees, the flowers,
The many-fruited bowers,
The lustred lilies and arboreal scent
And fresh young element
Of blood in every osseous vein of time,
New senses more sublime!
Should it not be that the ill days are past
And my soul lost at last,
Lost in thy bosom who art mother of all
Ere the first was, to fall
After the end. And then, O soul endued
(In this my solitude)
With all the thousand elements of life,
Shall I not call thee wife?
O must long wooed!
Long called to in the forest, on the mountain,
Reached after in the fountain,
Grasped in the slumberous sea,
And yet, ever, aye, ever! escaping me!

But here where the wise pen
And silver cadences outrunning song,
And clear sweet clean-chiselled English, sharp and strong,
Of the one man among the latter men

Orpheus

Who lived with Nature, saw her face to face,
And died not: here in this consummate place,
Immortal now, though the Antarctic sent
Its mightiest cold wave and rose and rent
The coral and annihilated land,
Or though the swarthy hand
Or foot misshapen of the Hephaestian,
(Hating the air-breathing man,
In such sweet love as dwells, above all other places
Here, in our hearts and faces,
Nature's and man's) if his coarse hand or foot,
The implacable forceful brute,
Shifted towards the bellows, and one blast
Blew through all the air aghast
And in one vast Titanic war,
Almighty avenging roar,
Oahu flung skywards blown in dust -- and was no more --
Even then immortal stands
This loveliest of all lands,
Lovelier even than they
Known in Elysian paths, heroic bands
Treading dim gardens brighter than the day,
Even in his voice who is passed, and shall no pass away!
Here therefore I know Nature: I am filled
With dew not earth-distilled
As I have prayed in vain, not vainly willed.
Now all the earth is stilled;
But ever the monotonous sea
Keeps solemn symphony,
Tuning my lyre to her own melody,
Not understandable in colder lands
Where no man understands
More than the mart; the raucous ironshod
Feet, smashing verses; the hard heavy hands
Of time: the hateful laugh where whoredom trod;
The savage snarl of man against his friend: --
How should he (such an one) perceive the end,
Or listen to the voice of Nature, know it for the voice of God?

EPODE.

NATURE.

Lo! in the interstellar space of night,
  Clothed with deep darkness, the majestic spaces
Abide the dawn of deity and light,
  Vibrate before the passionless pale faces
Shrined in exceeding glory, eremite.
  The tortoise skies in sombre carapaces
Await the expression and the hour of birth
In silence through the adamantine girth.

I rose in glory, gathered of the foam.

Aleister Crowley

The sea's flower folded, charioting me risen
Where dawn's rose stole from its pearl-glimmering home,
  And heaven laughed, and earth: and mine old prison,
The seas that lay beneath the mighty dome,
  Shone with my splendour. Light did first bedizen
Earth with its clusters of fiery dew and spray,
When I looked forth and cried "It is the day!"

The stars are dewdrops on my bosom's space;
  The sun and moon are glances through my lashes,
Long, tender, rays of night; my subtle face
  Burns through the sky-dusk, lightens, fills, and flashes
With solemn joy and laughter of love; the grace
  Of all my body swaying stoops and dashes
Swift to the daisy's dawn of love: and swiftest,
O spirit of man, when unto me thou liftest!

Dawn shakes the molten fire of my delight
  From the fine flower and fragrance of my tresses!
Sunset bids darken all my body's light,
  Mixing its music with the sad caresses
Of the whole world: I wheel in wingless flight
  Through lampless space, the starless wildernesses!
Beyond the universal bounds that roll,
There is the shrine and image of my soul.

Nature my name is called. O fruitless veil
  Of the strange self of its own self begotten!
O vision laughterless! O shadowy tale!
  O brain that halts before its thought forgotten!
Once all ye know me -- ere the earth grew pale,
  And Time began, and all its fruit lay rotten,
Once, when thou knewest me indeed, and fed
At these strong breasts -- Ah! but the days are dead!

Now, in the dusty corridors of Time,
  I am forgotten: Gaian language falters
If I would teach thee half an hint sublime
  Shed of the rayless fire upon my altars.
Vain are the light and laughter of man's rime,
  Vain the large hymns, and soaring songs and psalters!
My face, my breast, no soul of man uncovers,
Nor is my bed made lovely with my lovers!

I long for purple and the holier kiss
  Of mortal lyrist; in these arms to gladden;
To take him to the spring and source of bliss,
  And in his vast embrace to rouse me, madden
Once with the light of passion, not to miss
  Uttermost rapture till the sweet loves sadden
To sweeter peace thrilled with young ecstasy --
Ah! man's high spirit may not reach to Me!

Orpheus

I am Nature and God: I reign, I am, alone.
  None other may abide apart: they perish,
Drawn into me, into my being grown.
  None other bosom is, to bear, to nourish,
To be: the heart of all beneath my zone
  Of blue and gold is scarlet-bright to cherish
My own's life being, that is, and is not other;
For I am God and Nature and thy Mother.

I am the thousand-breasted milky spouse,
  Virginal also: Tartarus and Gaia
Twinned in my womb, and Chaos from my brows
  Shrank back abashed, my sister dark and dire,
Mother of Erebus and Night, that ploughs
  With starry-sandalled feet the fields of fire;
My sister shrank and fell, the infernal gloom
Changed to the hot sweet shadow of my womb.

I am: that darkness strange and uterine
  Is shot with dawn and scented with the rose;
The deep dim prison-house of corn and wine,
  Flowers, children, stars, with flame far subtler glows
Formless, all-piercing, death-defying, divine,
  A sweet frail lamp whose shadow gleams and shows
No darkness, is a light is where its rays
Cross, interweave, and marry with the day's!

I am: the heart that flames from central Me
  Seeks out all life, and takes again, to mingle
Its passion with my might and majesty,
  Till the vast floods of the man's being tingle
And glow, self-lost within my soul and sea
  Of love, and sun of utter light, and single
Keen many veined heart: our lips and kisses
Marry and muse on our immortal blisses.

I am: the greatest and the least: the sole
  And separate life of things. The mighty stresses
Of worlds are my nerves twitching. Branch and bole
  Of forests waving in deep wildernesses
Are hairs upon my body. Rivers roll
  To make one tear in my superb caresses,
When on myself myself begets a child,
A system of a thousand planets piled!

I am: the least, the greatest: the frail life
  Of some small coral-insect still may tremble
With love for me, and call me queen and wife;
  The shy plant of the water may dissemble
Its love beneath the fronds; reply to strife
  With strife, and all its tiny being crumble
Under my rough and warrior husband-kiss,
Whose pain shall burn, and alter, and be bliss!

Aleister Crowley

I am: no world beside that solemn one
  Reigns in sound's kingdom to express my station,
Who, clothed and crowned with suns beyond the sun,
  Bear on the mighty breast of foam Thalassian,
Bear on my bosom, jutting plenilune,
  Maiden, the fadeless Rose of the Creation!
The whole flower-life of earth and sky and sea
From me was born, and shall return to me!

I am: for men and beings passionate,
  For mine own self calm as the river-cleaving
Lotus-borne lord of Silence: I create
  Or discreate, both in my bosom heaving:
My lightest look is mother of a Fate:
  My fingers sapphire-ringed with sky are weaving
Ever new flowers and lawns of life, designed
Nobler and newer in mine olden mind.

I am: I am not, but all-changing move
  The worlds evolving in a golden ladder
Spiral or helical, fresh gusts of love
  Filling one sphere from the last sphere grown gladder;
All gateways leading far to the above.
  Even as the bright coils of the emerald adder
Climb one by one in glory of sunlight, climb
My children to me up the steep of Time.

I am: before me all the years are dead,
  And all the fiery locks of sunrise woven
Into the gold and scarlet of my head:
  In me all skies and seas are shaken and cloven:
All life and light and love about me shed
  Begotten in me, in my moving moven,
Are as my tears: all worlds that ever swam
As dew of kisses on my lips: I am.

But thou, chief lover, in whose golden heart
  The melody and music lifts its paean,
Whose lyre fulfilled of me, fathered of Art
  And that Sun's song beyond the Empyrean,
Who art myself, not any more apart,
  Having called my children by the call Pandean,
Mellowed with Delphian gold, the Ephesian quiver,
To float down Time for ever and for ever; --

I am thy lyre and thou mine harper: thou
  My music, I thy spirit: thou the lover
And I the bride: the glory of my brow
  Deeper delight, new ardour, to discover
Stoops in thine heart; my love and light endow
  Thy life with fervour as I bend me over
The starry curve and surface of the sea,

Orpheus

And kiss thy very life out into me.

O central fountain of my yearning veins!
  O mountain single-soaring, thou art blended
Into my heaven: prescient of the pains
  That shall bring forth -- what worlds? my heart is rended!
My womb reverberates the solar strains,
  The lyre vibrating in me: sharp and splendid
My face glows, gladdens; nuptial ecstasy
Is all the guerdon and the spoil of me!

I am: the universe grown old must bear
  A scion ere it sink to daedal slimber.
Thou art my strength, and I am only fair.
  Our kisses are as stars; our loves encumber
With multitude the fields of space, and where
  Our kisses tune the worlds, their lives outnumber
The moments of eternity: apart
I am for ever: and, in me, thou art!

EXPLICIT LIBER PRIMUS.

Aleister Crowley

LIBER SECUNDUS VEL AMORIS

TO

MARY BEATON

WHOM I LAMENT

"The Kabbalists say that when a man falls in love with a female elemental -- undine, sylph, gnome, or salamandrine, as the case may be -- she becomes immortal with him, or otherwise he dies with her.... The love of the magus for such beings is insensate, and may destroy him." -- *Eliphaz Levi.*

"Orpheus for the love he bare to his wife, snatcht, as it were, from him by untimely Death, resolved to go down to hell with his harp, to try if he might obtain her of the infernal power." -- *The Wisdom of the Ancients.*

ORPHEUS, FINDING EURYDICE DEAD, STUNG BY A SERPENT, LAMENTS OVER HER.

COME back, come back, come back, Eurydice!
    Come back to me!
Lie not so quiet, draw some faint sharp breath!
    It is not death:
It cannot, must not be, Eurydice.
    Come back to me!
Let me as yet lament not! Let me stoop! --
    Those eyelids droop
Not with mere death, but dreams, Eurydice!
    Come back to me!

O you that were my lover and my wife!
    Come back to life!
Come back, breathe softly from the breast of gold
    These arms enfold.
Give me your lips and kiss me once! O wife,
    Come back to life!
Nay, let the wind but stir the silky hair,
    (God's lesser air,
Not his full blossom of woman's breath!) O wife,
    Come back to life!

Stir once, move once, rise once, Eurydice!
    Be good to me!
Rise once. -- O sleep not! Listen! Is not all
    Nature my thrall?
Once only: be not dead, Eurydice!
    Be good to me!
I love you -- be not dead! -- rise up and say
    "I feigned, I lay

Orpheus

Thus so you kissed me" -- O Eurydice,
    Be good to me!

There is not one sweet sigh of all the old sighs --
    Open your eyes!
Not one warm breath of the young breast: no sleep
    Could be so deep.
The last pale lotus opens to the skies.
    Open your eyes!
Lift the blue eyelids under the deep lashes
    Till one light flashes!
Wake with one supreme sigh like the old sighs!
    Open your eyes!

I cannot leave you so, Eurydice.
    Come back to me!
Just in the triumph, in love's utmost hour,
    Life's queenliest flower --
All shattered, overblown. Eurydice,
    Come back to me!
I cannot have you dead, and live: let death
    Strangle my breath
Now as I kiss you still -- Eurydice!
    Come back to me!

Fling down the foolish lyre, the witless power!
Cast the dead laurel in the dust! The flower
  Of all the world is marred, the day's desire
Distorted in the eclipse, the sun's dead hour.

Let me fall down beside thee! Let me take
The kisses that thou canst not give, and slake
  Despair in purposeless caresses, dire
Shames fang-wise fastened of the eternal snake.

Is there no warmth where beauty is so bright?
No soul still flickering in the lambent light
  Still shed from all the body's excellence?
No lamp unchidden of the utter night?

Cannot my life be molten into thee,
Or thy death fall with rosier arms on me,
  Or soul with soul commingle without sense,
As the sun's rays strike deep into the sea?

O beauty of all beauty -- central flower
Of all the blossoms in the summer's bower!
  Fades not all nature in thy fall? the sun
Not darken in the miserable hour?

I hate all Nature's mockery of life.
The laugh is grown a grin; the gentle strife
  Of birds and waves and winds at play is grown

Aleister Crowley

A curse, a cruelty. My wife! my wife!

I am broken, I cannot sleep, I cannot die.
Pain, pain for ever! Nature is a lie,
　The gods a lie. Myself? but I am found
Sole serious in the hateful comedy.

Blackness, all blackness! How I hate the earth,
The curse that brought my being into birth.
　I, loving more her loveliness, am bound
And broken -- thrice more bitter for my mirth!

Song, was it song I trusted in? Or thou,
Apollo, was it thou didst bind my brow
　With laurel for a poison-wreath of hell
To sear my brain and blast my being now?

A band of most corroding poison wound
Dissolving with its venom the profound
　Deep of my spirit with its terrible
Sense without speech and horror without sound.

A devil intertwining in my heart
Its cold and hideous lust, a twiforked dart
　Even from the fatherly and healing hand --
The double death without a counterpart

In hell's own deepest pit, far, far below
Phlegethon's flame and Styx's stifling flow,
　Far below Tartarus, below the land
Thrust lowest in the devilish vertigo.

If I could weep or slumber or forget!
If love once left me, with his eyelids wet
　With tender memory of his own despair
Or frozen to a statue of regret!

If but the chilling agony, that turns
To bitter fever-heat that stings and burns
　Would freeze me, or destroy me, or impair
My sense, that it should feel not how it yearns!

Or if this pain were only pain, and not
A deadness deeper than all pain, a spot
　And central core of agony in me,
One heart-worm, one plague-leprosy, one blot

Of death, one anguish deeper than control? --
Then were I fit to gain the Olympian goal
　And fling forth fiery wailings to the sea,
And tune the sun's ray to my smitten soul!

How should I sing who cannot even see?

Orpheus

Grope through a mist of changless misery.
 An age-long pain -- no time in wretchedness! --
As of an hammer annihilating me

With swift hard rhythm, the remorseless clang;
Or as a serpent loosening his fang
 To bite more deeply -- this inane distress
More than despair or death's detested pang.

I live -- that shames me! I am not a man.
Nothing can I to sharpen or to span
 My throat with iron fingers, or my sword
In my heart's acid where the blood began

Long since to leap, and now drops deadly slow,
Clotted with salt and sulphur and strong woe.
 I shall not die: the first sight of the sward
Stained with the spectral corpse had stung me so,

Not stabbed me, since I saw her and survive.
I shall not die -- Ah! shall I be alive?
 This hath no part in either: bale and bliss
Forget me, careless if I rot or thrive.

Heaven forgot me -- or she were not dead!
And Hades -- or I should not raise my head
 Now, and look wildly where I used to kiss,
Gaze on the form whence all but form has fled!

I am alone in all the universe,
Changed to the shape and image of a curse,
 Muffled in self-confusion, and my brain
Wakes not nor sleeps: its destiny is worse.

It thinks not, knows not, acts not, nor appeals,
But hangs, remembers: it abides and feels
 As if God's vulture clung to it amain,
And furies fixed with fiery darts and wheels

Their horror, thought-exceeding, manifold,
Vertiginous within me -- and the cold
 Of Styx splashed on me, making me immortal,
Invulnerable in its bitter mould;

Leaving its own ice, penetrating streams,
Grim streaks, and dismal drops, abysmal beams
 Thrown from the gulph through the place and portal,
Each drop o'erladen with a curse that steams

Unnatural in the coldness: let me be
Alone, inviolate of eternity!
 Let all the winds of air leave me, nor fan:
Nor wash me all the waves of all the sea!

Aleister Crowley

Let all the sun's light and the moon's be blind,
And all the stars be lampless to my mind,
  Until I see the destiny of man
And span the cruelty that lurks behind

Its beauty, and its glory, and its splendour! --
The girl-babe's face looks up to the mother tender,
  Looks for a kiss in dumb desire, and finds
Her Jaws closed trap-like to expunge and end her!

Let all the life and dream and death be done,
And all the love and hate be woven in one,
  All things be broken of the winter winds,
No soul stand up and look upon the sun!

Save only mine! -- that my voice may confound
The universe, and spell the mighty sound
  To shake all heaven and earth, to mingle hell
In chaos, in some limitless profound;

That it may tear Olympus from its place,
Mix it with Hades, change the Ocean space,
  Level the tides of time that sink and swell,
And curse my very father to his face!

O father, father Apollo, did I wrong
Thy chariot and thy horses in my song?
  Why clove thine arrow the unseated air,
The heaven void of thee, why the thunderthong

Slipped from the tether, and the fatal stone
Sped not to my heart, not to mine alone?
  Ah why not? but to hers as she lay sleeping
By hate, not fate, quelled, fallen, and overthrown?

She lies so pitiful and pure -- and I,
Breast to her breast, mouth to her mouth, I lie,
  Hand upon hand, and foot on foot, sore weeping --
Can she not live again or I not die?

As the old prophet on the child I fall
And breathe -- but no breath answers me at all.
  All of my kisses stir no blush, no sigh;
She will not hear me ever if I call!

Let the far music of oblivious years
  Sound in the sea beneath!
Are not its waters one with all my tears?
Hath Atropos no comfort in her shears?
  No Muse for me one wreath?

Were I now dead and free to travel far

Orpheus

Whither I will, ah me!
Not whither I must -- were there no avatar
Drawn like my love from some close kindred star?
No shape seen on the sea?

Were I now free of this intense desire,
  By swift magician power
I might fly westward shod with wings of fire
And find my love, and in her arms expire,
  Or wed her for an hour.

(Not for an hour as man, but even as God
  Whose day is like an aeon.
Love hath nor station, stage, nor period:
But is at once in his inane abode
  Beneath the spring Dircean.)

Alas, the will flies ere the power began.
  Lo, in the Idan grove
Invoking Zeus to swell the power of Pan,
The prayer discomfits the demented man!
  Lust lies as still as love.

Therefore in memory only is there life,
  And in sweet shapes of art:
The same thought for the ointment and the knife --
Oh lightning! blast the image of my wife
  Out of my mind and heart!

How can one hour dissolve a year's delight?
One arrow striking the full eagle-flight
  Drop him so swift, giving no time to die,
No dusk to hearld and delay the night?

A serpent stung her sleeping: if the abyss
Know any cell more dolorous than this,
  Were there a sharper tooth to destiny
Than this that strikes me in the dead girl's kiss: --

Oh if aught bitterer could be, could know,
If ninefold Styx could gather in its flow
  Cocytus, Phlegethon, and Acheron,
All mixed to one full flood of hate and woe:

And poisoned by all venom like to his
Who kissed Eurydice the traitor-kiss: --
  Then let them sting me four fold, nor atone
Then for the eightfold misery of this!

Is not some justice somewhere? Where is he
Hateful to God and man, a misery
  To his own vileness by exceeding it,
Who crawls God-cursed throughout eternity

Aleister Crowley

Nay! sure he lives, and licks his slavered lips,
Laughing to think how the sweet morsel slips,
　The breast-flower of my bride; the dainty bit
Fit for -- ah God! the pearl-smooth blossom drips

Poisonous blood that will not poison me,
Though I drink deep its fierce intensity.
　My lips closed silent on her bosom's light,
The stung blood springs -- like pearls beneath the sea

Whose moony glimmer hath a purple vein
Hidden -- so I athirst of the said stain
　Drink up her body's life, as if to spite
Its quiet, as if the venom were to drain

Into my life -- that hurts me not at all,
Struck by a stronger buffet: let me call
　All deaths! they come not, seeing I am broken
In this one horror where a man may fall.

I am alive, and live not: I am dead,
And die not: on my desolated head
　No dew may drop, no word of God be spoken,
None heard, if by some chance some word be said.

The wheels of Fate are over me; quite crushed
Lies my pale body where her body blushed,
　Quite dead! there is no single sob that stirs,
No pulse of blood of all that filled and flushed

Her cheek and mine, her breast and mine: and lo!
How sunset's bloom is faded on the snow!
　There is no laugh of all those laughs of hers,
Those tender thrills of laughter I used to know.

Nor in all nature weep the careless eyes,
Nor any soul of life may sympathise,
　All I once was in this is torn and rended --
Scorned and forsaken the lone lyre lies.

Hath that not yet some sympathy with me?
That lyre that was myself, my heart's decree
　And ruler, subtle at the dawn, and splendid
Noonwards, and soft at day's declivity!

I flung it in my anguish to the ground.
I raise it, and its music hath not found
　One string or snapped or loosened, and the tune
Is the old triumph garlanded and crowned!

Folly and hate! Blithe mockery of sorrow!
Shrill me no harsh lies of some sweet tomorrow!

Orpheus

Soothe me no hateful mysteries of the moon,
How one life lends what other lives may borrow!

I hate that foolish counterfoil of grief
That one pain to its friend may give relief --
  Eurydice replace Eurydice
Long hence -- no separation sharp and brief

But dwelling in the intermediate
Halls between Hades and the house of Fate:
  Atropos cut, and pass to Clotho, and she
Respin the shuttle in some other state.

What shall it boot me now to gather flowers
From this young hope to wile the angry hours?
  That many thousand years shall pass, and show
Eurydice again amid her bowers.

Forgetting, and myself again be born,
Clasp her grave beauty in the middle corn,
  Forgetting also: Time as fallen snow
Blotting the mind and memory that adorn

At least our present littleness: nor hope
Of larger excellence, extended scope,
  Shall help me here, forgetting: nothing skills
Of this poor truth -- to flatter with the trope!

Wooing in mockery! -- nothing skills but this
To raise her now, and resuspire the kiss
  United by the splendour of the will's
Success -- to marry, to be made of bliss,

I care not whether there or there: to live
In memory and identity: to give
  No part of self or soul to Lethe's water:
To grapple Nature, interpose an "if"

In her machinery of conditioned mood;
Suspending law, suspending amplitude
  Of all Her function; to espouse her daughter
In forced embrace lasciviously rude,

Indecorous, shameful to the eternal "must"!
Law may be mercy, mercy never just!
  Thus I would alter, and divide her ways,
And let her wheels grind themselves down to dust.

One supernatural event -- but one! --
Should scale Olympus, shattering the throne
  Of the Ægis-bearing Father: and the days
Of all the Universe be fallen and done.

Well then? O sceptred Splendour! dost Thou see
How little means Thy Universe to Me?
  How petty looks Thy will to My desire?
Hebe and Hera to Eurydice?

I, knowing all the progress of the earth,
The dim procession, altering death and birth,
  The Seven Stairs, the gusts of life in fire
And Love in Life, and all the serpent girth

Of sevenfold twining worlds and sevenfold ways
And nights made sevenfold of the sevenfold days
  All the vast scheme evolving into man,
And upward, onward, through Olympian haze

Into the crowning spiritual mist,
Where spirit in the spirit may subsist,
  Evolve itself in the amazing plan
Through many planes, as shining amethyst

Melts to the sapphire's sombre indigo,
And lifts, still sapphire, to the ocean glow;
  Thence into emerald and the golden light,
Till ruby crown the river's living flow

And glory of colour in the sun's own flame --
Beyond, to colours without sense or name,
  Impossible to man, whose vivid sight
Would blast him with their splendour as they came

Flashing through spiritual space, withdrawn
Now, and now flung triumphant in the dawn
  Not of mere sun's rise, but before the birth
Of a new system on the unfolded lawn

Of space beyond the sceptre of the Gods!
I, seeing all this would foil Time's periods
  For one small woman on this one mean earth,
Would spoil the plan of the inane Abodes,

Throw out of gear all Nature's enginery
For such a grain of tinsel dust as I,
  Reluctant to be mangled in the wheel --
Looks other meanness so contemptibly?

Yet I persist. Thou knowest, O most High Zeus,
When Hera to thine Io did refuse
  Peace, and the gadfly bit like barbed steel
Those limbs with dews of love once lying loose,

When thy vast body boarded her, wrapped round
Her senses with a mist of being profound,

Orpheus

A flame-like penetration, serpentine,
Twining and leaping without end or bound,

Inevitable as the gasp of Fate: --
Thou, reft of her by envy of thy mate
  Didst shake the heaven with bellowings undivine,
And rooted stars from their primeval state.

Not without law, sayest thou? Almighty Zeus,
Am I not also mothered of a Muse?
  Let there be law! untimely to release
This soul untinctured of the Stygian dews,

Unsprinkled of Lethean lotus-drops!
Life grows so steadily, so sudden stops --
  (Surely no part in Nature's moving peace!)
Thus, when the young, like tempest-stricken crops

Unripe, are blasted in the blossoming spring --
This is a miracle, not the other thing!
  Nature insults herself, blasphemes her God,
Thus cutting short the life's hard happening.

Nor would I suffer thus, nor she repine
Had my wife faded (as rose-tinted wine
  Bleached in the sunlight) reached her period
And fallen gently in the arms divine,

Caressing arms of pale Persephone,
And bathed her in death's river tenderly,
  Washing the whole bright body, the long limbs,
The clothing hair, the face, the witchery

Of all the smiling shape in the dark stream,
As one who gathers the first floral beam
  Of daylight by the water, dives and swims
Deep in cool alleys, softer than a dream:

So, rising to the other bank, aglow
With the bright motion and the stream's young flow,
  She might discover the Elysian ground,
And find me waiting, find me sad and slow

Pacing the green flower-lighted turf, and leap
Into my body's kisses, into sleep: --
  Sweeter this latter bridal than we found
The first, now lost in time's eternal deep.

It is not cruel if the ripe fruit fall --
But never an elegy funereal
  Wept for untimely burial, but cried
Aloud against the Fates, forebore to call

Aleister Crowley

In pity or passion on the Gods of peace;
But cursed, but wailed, nor bade its sharp tongue cease
  Until lightning spat, sharp to divide
Bone from its marrow for their blasphemies!

So I should curse, unless indeed my grief
Be not to great to yield me such relief.
  Methinks a sob must start and mar the roar
Of loud harsh laughing bitter unbelief

Scarring the sky with poisonous foam of song.
Also, what curse might remedy the wrong?
  Are not all feuds forgotten in a war?
All stars exhausted in Astraea's throng

When the swift sun leaps skyward? Let me speak
Words rather of wisdom: hate may rage and wreak
  Vengeance in vain if wisdom smile beyond,
Too high to care, too ultimate to seek.

The bitterest sorrow of all sorrow is this:
I had no time to catch one last long kiss,
  Nor bid farewell, nor lay one lily-frond
Of resurrection for the sign of bliss,

Remembrance of some immortality
Affirmed if not believed: alas for me
  That might not interchange the last sad vows,
Nor close the blue eyes clearer than the sea

Before they darkened, and the veil of death
Shrouded their splendour: still there lingereth
  Some sad white lustre on the icy brows,
Some breast-curve surely indicating breath,

Some misty glamour of deep love within
The eye's cold gleam! some dimple on the chin
  Hinting of laughter: even now she seems
A folded rosebud, where the ivory skin

Closes the ripe warm centre flower, the mind,
The spirit that was beautifully kind,
  The sense of beauty shadowed in deep dreams,
Sent though the horn gates by some sleepy wind.

All lingers: all is gone: a little while,
And all the live sweet rapture of the smile
  Of her whole being is discomfited,
The body broken, desolated, vile,

Till nought remains but the memorial urn
Of deep red gold, less golden than did burn
  Once the strong breast: the ash within is shed,

Orpheus

Dust given for flowers: what memory shall turn

Unto the flowers, think worthy to remember
How the dust scattered from their fading ember
  Is their own sign and seal of fatherhood,
Grey seas of sorrow sun-kissed into amber.

Above me hangs the sun: horrid he hangs,
A rayless globe of hell, shooting forth fangs
  Snake-wise to parch and burn my solitude,
Nor leave me quiet lamenting, with these pangs

Tearing my live, more Promethean
Than ever Titan knew -- the sunbright span
  Of narrow water mocks me, brightening
Far to the indigo Ionian.

The sun hangs high, as in the Arabian tale
Enchanted palaces defy the gale,
  Perched upon airy mountains, on the wing
Of genii poised, souls suffering and pale

With their long labour: wizard spire and dome
That maidens grown magicians had for home,
  Where the charmed sword and graven talisman
Held them supremely floating on the foam

Where cloudier seas innavigably roll,
Misty with elemental shape or soul,
  This grey essential nebulae of man,
Caught in the mesh of magical control!

All these are beautiful and shapen so
That every bastion flames a separate glow
  Of changing colour: all detestable,
Abhorrent, since the goodly-seeming show

Is one large lie of cruelty and lust,
Carven from the spectral images of dust,
  Founded on visions of the accursed well,
And built of shame and hatred and distrust,

And all things hateful and all lying things --
O song! where wanderest on forgetful wings?
  Shall these wild numbers help thee to thine own,
Or change the winter's gramarye to spring's?

Rather beguile the tedious mourning hours
With memory of the long-forgotten bowers,
  Where loves resurged from cave and grove to throne,
From nuptial banquet to the bed of flowers!

Rather forget the near catastrophe,

Aleister Crowley

And turn my music toward Eurydice;
  Awake in day-dream all the ancient days,
When love first blossomed on the springing tree!

Let me recall the days beyond regret,
And tune my lyre to love, sharpen and set
  The strings again to the forgotten ways,
That I may tread them over, and forget!

In child-like meditative mood
  I wandered in the dell,
Passed through the quiet glades of the wood,
  And sought the haunted well,
Half hopeful that its solitude
  Might work some miracle.

The oaks raised angry hands on high:
  The willows drooped for tears:
The yews held solemn ceremony,
  Magical spells of years.
I saw one cypress melancholy,
  A prince among his peers.

So, turning from the arboreal seat
  And midmost hollow of earth,
I followed Hamadryads' feet
  That made at eve their mirth
To where the streamlet wandered fleet
  To show what time was worth.

I watched the waters wake and laugh
  Running o'er pebbly beaches,
Writing amazement's epitaph
  With freshets, turns, and reaches: --
The only tale too short by half
  That nature ever teaches.

Then growing grander as it swept
  Past bulrushes and ferns,
Gathering the tears that heaven had wept,
  The water glows and burns
In sunlight, where no shadows crept
  Around the lazy turns.

All on a sudden silence came
  Athwart some avenue
Where through the trees arrowed the flame
  From the exultant blue;
And all the water-way became
  One heart of glittering dew.

The waters narrowed for a space
  Between twin rocks confined,

Orpheus

Carven like Gods for poise and grace,
  Like miracles for mind:
Each fashioned like a kissing face,
  The eyes for joy being blind.

The waters widened in a pool,
  Broad mirror of blue light.
The surface was as still and cool
  As the broad-breasted night.
Engraven of no mortal tool,
  The granite glistened white.

As if to shield from mortal gaze
  A nymph's immortal limbs,
The shadow of the buttress stays
  And dips its head and swims,
While moss engirdles it with grays
  And greens that dew bedims.

Now, at the last, the western end,
  Most miracle of all!
The groves of rock dispart and rend
  Their sacred cincture-wall;
All tunes of heaven their rapture lend
  To make the waterfall.

There, streaming from the haze and mist
  Where dew is dashed in spray,
Rises a halo sunrise-kissed
  And kissed at close of day
From ruby unto amethyst,
  Within the veil of grey.

And there within the circled light
  I saw a dancing thing,
Most like the tender-leaved night
  Of moonrise seen in spring,
A shadow luminous and white
  Like a ghost beckoning.

And then dim visions came to me,
  Faint memories of fear:
As when the Argo put on sea
  Such stories we did hear,
Stories to tremble at and flee --
  And others worth a tear.

I thought of how a maiden man
  Might hear a deadly song
And clasp a siren in his span,
  And feel her kiss grow strong
To drag him with caresses wan
  Into the House of Wrong.

Another: how the women grew
  Like vines of tender grape,
And how they laughed as lovers do,
  And took a lover's shape,
And how men sought them, free to woo --
  To leave them, no escape!

Another: how a golden cup
  A golden girl would pour,
And whoso laughed and drank it up
  Grew wise and warrior:
But whoso stayed to smile and sup
  Returned -- ah, never more!

And yet again -- a river steep,
  A maiden combing light,
Her hair's enchantment -- she would weep
  And sing for love's delight,
Until the listener dropped to sleep
  In magic of her night.

And then the maiden smoothed her tresses,
  And led him to the river,
Caught him and kissed with young caresses,
  And then -- her cruel smiles quiver!
Beneath the waves his life represses
  For ever and for ever!

I knew the danger of the deed
  The while enrapt I gladdened.
My eyes upon the dancer feed
  As one by daylight saddened
After long night whose slumbers bleed,
  By dreams deceived and maddened!

It might be -- the delusive dance,
  The shadowy form I saw,
Apollo's misty quivering lance
  Thrown to elude God's law;
It might be -- doth the maid advance,
  Evanish, or withdraw?

So stung by certainty's mistrust,
  Or tranced in dream of sin,
Or blinded by some Panic dust,
  By Dionysian din
Deafened, arose the laughing lust
  To fling my body in!

I stood upon the rock, and cried,
  And held my body high
(Not caring if I lived or died)

Orpheus

Erect against the sky:
Then plunged into the wheeling tide,
And vanished utterly.

"O shape half-seen of love, and ost
  Beneath time's sightless tide,
What obolus of the vital cost
  Remains, or may abide?
Or what perception memory steal,
Once passed upon the whirling wheel?

"O hope half held of love, and fled
  Beyond the ivory gate,
A dream gone from the hapless head
  By fury of a fate!
What image of the hope returns
But stings with agony that which yearns?

"O face half kissed in faith and fear,
  Eager and beautiful!
Drop for mortality one tear!
  For life one smile recall!
There is no passion made for me --
Else were my water-well the sea."

Such tune my falling body snapped
  Within the sacred sides,
While the warm waves with laughter lapped,
  And changed their tuned tides,
And all my being was enwrapped,
  A bridegroom's in the bride's.

Deep in the hollow of the place
  A starry bed I saw,
Gemmed with strange stones in many a space
  Of godlike rune and law.
Such fancies as the fiery face
  Of living Art might draw.

But rising up I lift my head
  Beyond the ripples clean:
My arms with spray dew-diamonded
  Stretched love-wise to my queen
That danced upon the light, and shed
  Her own sweet light between.

But never a mortal joy might know,
  Hold never a mortal lover!
Whose limbs like moonshine glint and glow,
  Throb, palpitate, and hover: --
Pale sunrise woven with the snow
  Athwart a larchen cover!

So danced she in the rainbow mist,
  A fairy frail and chaste,
By moon caressed, by sunlight kissed
  A guerdon vain and waste;
And the misery of her thankless tryst
  Stole on me as she paced.

For never her lips should be caressed
  By love's exulting stings,
Whose starry shape shone in the west,
  Held of the glimmering wings.
Her shadowy soul perceived the jest
  Of man and mortal things.

And there I vowed a solemn oath
  To Aphrodite fair,
Sealing that sacramental troth
  With a long curl of hair,
And the strange prayer's reiterant growth
  Sent shining through the air.

(*Invoking Aphrodite*)

    Daughter of Glory, child
    Of Earth's Dione mild
By the Father of all, the Ægis-bearing King!
    Spouse, daughter, mother of God,
    Queen of the blest abode
In Cyprus' splendour singly glittering.
    Sweet sister unto me,
    I cry aloud to thee!
I laugh upon thee laughing, O dew caught up from sea!

    Drawn by sharp sparrow and dove
    And swan's wide plumes of love,
And all the swallow's swifter vehemence,
    And, subtler than the Sphinx,
    The ineffable iynx
Heralds thy splendour swooning into sense,
    When from the bluest bowers
    And greenest-hearted hours
Of Heaven thou smilest toward earth, a miracle of flowers!

    Down to the loveless sea
    Where lay Persephone
Violate, where the shad of earth is black,
    Crystalline out of space
    Flames the immortal face!
The glory of the comet-tailed track
    Blinds all black earth with tears.
    Silence awakes and hears
The music of thy moving come over the starry spheres.

Orpheus

    Wrapped in rose, green and gold,
    Blues many and manifold,
A cloud of incense hides thy splendour of light;
    Hides from the prayer's distress
    Thy loftier loveliness
Till thy veil's glory shrouds the earth from night;
    And silence speaks indeed,
    Seeing the subtler speed
Of its own thought than speech of the Pandean reed!

    There no voice may be heard!
    No place for any word!
The heart's whole fervour silently speeds to thee,
    Immaculate! and craves
    Thy kisses or the grave's,
Till, knowing its unworthiness to woo thee,
    Remembers, grows content
    With the old element,
And asks the lowlier grace its earlier music meant.

    So, Lady of all power!
    Kindle this firstling flower
The rainbow nymph above the waterfall
    Into a mortal shade
    Of thee, immortal maid,
That in her love I gather and recall
    Some memory mighty and mute
    In love's poor substitute
Of thee, thy Love too high, the impossible pursuit!

    Then from the cloud a golden voice
      Great harmonies persuade,
    That all the cosmic lawns rejoice
      Like laughter of a maid;
    Till evolution had no choice
      But heard it, and obeyed.

    "Show by thy magic art
      The hero-story!
    Awake the maiden heart
      With tunes of glory!
    With mortal joys and tears,
      Keen woes and blisses,
    Awake her faiths and fears,
      Her tears and kisses!"

    I caught the lavish lyre, and sate
      Hard by the waterfall,
    Twisting its sweetness intimate
      Into the solemn call
    Of many dead men that were great,

The plectron's wizard thrall.

Thus as she danced, nor ceased, nor cared,
  I set the sacred throng
Of heroes into acts that fared
  In Argo light and long,
The foes they fought, the feats they dared,
  In shadow-show and song.

(*The play of Argonautae is shadowed before them by Orpheus' magical might.*)

So faded all the dream: so stole
Some fearful fondness in her soul;
Even as a cloud thrilled sharply through
With lightning's temper keen and true,
Splitting the ether: so again
Grew on me the ecstatic pain,
Seeing her tremble in mid-air.
No flower so exquisitely fair
Shakes out its petals at the dawn;
No breath so beautiful is drawn
At even by the listening vale.
For oh! she trembled! Frail and pale,
Her looks surpassing loveliness
Lulled its own light to fond distress,
As if the soul were hardly yet
Fit to remember or forget
New-born! and though the goddess bade
The nymph-bud blossom to a maid,
And soulless immortality
Reach to a soul, at last to die,
For love's own sake, bliss dearly bought
For change's altering coin ill-wrought,
It seemed as through the soul were strange,
Not fledged, not capable to range
At random through the world of sense
Opened so swift and so intense
Unto the being. Thus she stood
Impatient on the patient flood
With wonder waking in her eyes.
Thus the young dove droops wing, and dies,
In wonder why the winged thing
Loosed from yon twanging silver string
Should strike, should hurt. But now she wakes,
Wreathes like a waterfall of snakes
The golden fervour of her hair
About the body brave and bare
Starred in the sunlight by the spray,
And laughed upon me as I lay
Watching the change: First dawn of fire!
First ghost of nightfall's grey desire!
First light of moonrise! Then, as June
Leaps out of May, her lips took tune

Orpheus

To song most soft, a spiral spell,
As siren breathing in a shell.
The notes were clustered round the well
Like angels clustering round a god.
Let memory wake from its abode
Of dim precision lost for long
The grace and grandeur of the song!

Who art thou, love, by what sweet name I quicken?
By whom, O love, my soul is subtly stricken?
   O Love, O Love, I linger
On the dear word and know not any meaning,
Nor why I chant; there is a whisper weaning
My soul from depths I knew to depths I guess,
Centred in two words only: "Love" and "Yes."
   What lyrist's gentle finger
Strikes out a note, a key, a chord unheard of?
What voice intones a song I know no word of?
   Who am I, Love, and where?
What is the wonder of this troublous singing?
What is the meaning of my spirit's clinging
Still to the two sweet words: repeat, repeat!
"Yes, Love!" and "Yes, Love!" Oh the murmur sweet!
   The fragrance in the air!
I know not, I; amid the choral gladness
Steals an essential tremor as of sadness,
   A grace-note to the bosom
Of music's spell that binds me, as in Panic
Dance to some grasp unthinkable, Titanic,
Unto the words fresh flowers that distil
Uttermost fragrance in the mind and will,
   The unsuspected blossom!
What is the change -- new birth of spring-time kisses
Alone in all these water-wildernesses?
   What change? what loveliness!
Comes this to all? I heard my sisters crying
No tale like this -- O! were I only lying
Asleep amid the ferns, my soul would weep
Over and over in its endless sleep;
   "Yes, love!" and "yes!" and "yes!"

So by some spell divinely drawn
She came to me across the dawn,
With open arms to me; and sobbed
"Yes, love!" and "Yes, love!" O how throbbed
The giant glory at my heart!
And I? I drew away, apart,
Lest by mere chance to me she came.
But curling as a wind-blown flame
She turned, she found me. As the dew
Melts in the lake's dissolving blue

So to my arms she came. And now,
Now, now I hold her!
                    Broke the brow
Of all wide heaven in thunder! Hear
Tremendous vortices of fear
Swirl in the ether. What new terror
Darkens the blue pool's sliver mirror?
How bursts the mountain-chasm asunder?
Whose voice reverberates in thunder
Muttering what curse? The sun dissolves
In anguish; the mad moon revolves
Like a wild thing about its cage;
The stars are shaken in the rage
Of -- who but Zeus? Before our gaze,
(My love's in shuddering amaze,
Of birth deceived and death forlorn,
And mine in anger, ay! and scorn!)
He stood -- the mighty One! So earth
And heaven proclaimed that fearful birth:
So they grew silent lest he curse.
Dead silence hushed the universe;
And then in clear calm tones he spoke:
"Fools! who have meddled, and awoke
The inmost forces of the world!
One lightning from my hand had hurled
Both to annihilation's brink.
What foolish goddess bade ye think
Ye thus could play with thunder, roll
Your wheels upon the world, control
The stately being of a soul?
Just am I ever! Therefore know
The unrevengeful law of woe
That ye invoke. Thou seekest life,
Child of my water! Thou a wife,
Child of my sun! Draw living breath,
Maiden, and gain the guerdon -- death!
Thou take the wife, and risk the fate
Æons could hardly culminate
To lose thy soul! Not two but one
Are ye. Together, as the stone,
The oak, the river, or the sea,
Mere elements of mine be ye,
Or both resolve the dreadful life,
And take death's prize! Take thou the wife,
Thou, who didst know. Her ignorance
Resolve itself upon a chance!
She shall decide the double fate.
Be still, my child, and meditate!
This is an hour in heaven." He ceased
And I was silent. she released
Her soul from that tremendous birth
Of fear in gentle-minded mirth.
"Great Sir!" she cried, "the choice is made!

Orpheus

An hour ago I was afraid,
Knew nothing, and loved not. But I
Know now not this you say -- to die.
Some doubtful change! An hour ago
I was a nymph. I did not know
This change: but now for death or life
I care not. Am I not his wife?
I love him. Now I would not leave
That joy once tasted; shall not grieve
If even that should ever cease,
So great a pleasure (and a peace!)
I have therein. And by the sense
Of love's intuitive influence
I know he wills me to remain
Woman." "How frivolous and vain,
O Zeus," I cried, "art thou to rise
Out of Olympus' ecstasies!
Omnipotent! but to control
The first breath of a human soul! --"
The thunder rolled through heaven again,
Void was the spring-delighted plain
Of that gigantic phantasy.
I turned to my Eurydice
Even as she turned. The faint breath glows, --
The lightning of a living rose.
The bright eyes gleam -- night's spotless stars
Glimmering through folded nenuphars.
The red mouth moves, still to the word:
"Yes, love!" and "yes, love!" Then I heard
No sound and saw no sight -- the world
Folded its mighty wings, and curled
Its passion round us; bade forget
The joy with which our eyes were wet.
All faded, folded in the bliss;
Unfolded the first fadeless kiss.

Then my soul woke, not sundering lips,
But winged against the black eclipse
Of sense: my soul on wings did poise
Her glory in the vast turquoise
Of the whole sky: expanded far
Beyond the farthest sun or star,
Beyond all space, all time. I saw
The very limits of the law
That hath no bounds: beheld the bliss
Of that first wonder of the kiss
In its true self: how very love
Is God, and hath its substance of
Pure light: and how love hath its cause
Beyond religions, worlds, and laws;
Is in itself the first: and moves
All evolution, and disproves
God in affirming God: all this

In that one rapture of the kiss
I knew, and all creation's pain
Fell into nothing in my brain,
As I, remaining man, involved
All life's true purpose, and dissolved
The phantoms (of itself create)
In a mysterious sweet state,
Wherein some tune began to move
Whose likeness and whose life was love.

Roll, strong life-current of these very veins,
  Into my lover's soul, my soul that is!
Thrill, mighty life of nerves, exultant strains
Triumphant of all music in a kiss!
    Fade! fade, oh strenuous sense
    Into the soul intense
Of life beyond your weak imagining!
    And, O thou thought, dissever
    Thy airy life for ever
While the bright sounds are lifted up to spring
    Beyond this tide of being,
    Shadows and sense far fleeing
Into a shadow deeper than the Ocean
  When passes all the mind's commotion
To a serener sky, a mighty calm emotion!

The whole world fades, folds over its wide pinions
  Into a darkness deeper than its own.
Silence hath shattered all the dream-dominions
  Of life and light: the grey bird's soul is flown
    Into a soundless night,
    Lampless: a vivid flight
Beyond the thrones and stars of heaven down hurled,
    Till the great blackness heaves
    An iron breast, and cleaves
The womb of night, another mightier world.
    Lost is my soul, and faded
    The light of life that braided
  Its comet tresses into golden fire.
    Fade, fade, the phantoms of desire!
Speed, speed the song of love upon the living lyre!

Lo! I abide not, and my lover's glory
  Abides not: in the swaying of those tides
Gathers beneath some mighty promontory
  One mightier wave, deep drowns it, and abides.
    Save that one wave alone
    Nought in the void is known,
That wave of love, that sole exultant splendour
    Throned o'er all being, supreme,
    A single-shining beam
  Burning with love, unutterably tender.
    Ah! the calm wave retires.

Orpheus

Down all the fearful fires
Go thundering to darkness, so dissever
Their being from pure being, that the river
Of love is waveless now, and is pure love for ever.

Then mightier than all birth of stars or suns,
  Breaks the vast flood and trembles in its tide.
Serene an splendid shine the mystic ones,
  Exult, appal, reiterate, abide.
   Timid and fleet the earth
  Comes rushing back to birth,
Brighter and greener, radiant with gold
  Of a diviner sun,
  An exultation
Of life to life, of light to light untold.
   I? I remain, and see
  Across eternity
My lover's face, and gaze, and know the worth
Of love's life to the glowing earth,
The kiss that wakes all life unto a better birth.

So the swoon broke. I saw the face
(Shining with Love's reverberant grace)
Of my own love across the lawn,
As warm and tender as the dawn
Tinting the snows of heaven-born hills,
Enamelling the mountain rills
With light's chameleon-coloured dyes;
So shone the love-light in grey eyes,
Changing for laughter and for tears,
Changeless for joy of myriad years.
This, this endures; there is no lover,
No loved one; all the ages cover
These things from sight: but this abides
Floating above the whelming tides
Of time and space: abides for ever
Whether the lovers join or sever.
There is no change: the love exists
Beyond the moment's suns and mists
in me, abiding: and I see
No lover in Eurydice,
Save that her kiss awoke in me
This knowledge, this supreme content,
Annihilation of the event,
The vast eternal element
Of utter being, bliss, and thought,
In dissolution direly wrought
Of sense, identity's eclipse,
The shadow of a lover's lips.
The awful steel of Death divides
The alternation of the tides
Of consciousness, and binds in bliss
The dead man to the girl's live kiss.

So sped my wooing: now I surely think
Suspended here upon the burning brink
  Of this dim agony, invading sense,
That bliss should still abide: but now I shrink,

Fall from the crags of memory, and abide
Now in this nature-life, basilisk-eyed,
  And serpent-stinging: yea, I perish thence.
That perishes which was: and I am tied

Unto myself: the "I" springs up again
Bound to the wheel of speedless sense and pain,
  None loosing me. Past is the utter bliss;
Present the strong fact of the death, the stain

Of the marred lives: I meditate awhile
Not on the mere light of the girl, the smile
  Deepening down to the extremest kiss;
Not of the long joys of the little isle

Set in Ionian waters, where the years
Passed, one long passion, too divine for tears,
  Too deep for laughter: but on that divine
Sense beyond sense, the shadow of the spheres

Lost in the all-pervading light of love:
That bliss all passion and all praise above;
  Impersonal, that fervour of the shrine
Changed to pure peace that had its substance of

Nothing but love: in vain my thoughts evoke
That light amidst the deadly night and smoke
  Of this dread hour: there's nothing serves nor skills
Here, since that hateful "I" of me awoke,

Making me separate from the wings of life.
Nothing avails me of the cruel strife
  With my own being: hideous sorrow fills
My heart -- O misery! my wife! my wife!

Stay! if I cannot be the Absolute,
Let me be man! discard the wailing lute
  And wake the lyre: the mightier than me
Drag up the courage in me to dispute

The battle with despair: awake the strings
Stronger than earth, than the immortal kings
  Alike of death and life: invoke the sea
That I may cross her on the viewless wings

Of song, find out the desolating river

Orpheus

That girds the earth, unloose the silver quiver,
  Choosing an arrow of sharp song to run
Down to the waters that lament for ever: --

And cleave them! That my song's insistent spell
Rive the strong gates of iron-builded hell,
  And move the heart of the ill-hearted one.
Yea! let me break the portals terrible,

And bring her back! come back, Eurydice!
Come back, pale wanderer to Eternity!
  Come back, my wife, my wife, again to love!
Come back, my wife! come back, come back to me!

Enough! my purpose holds: no feeble cries!
No sob shall shake these nerves: no ecstasies
  Of hope, or fear, or love avail to move
Those iron-hearted dooms and destinies.

I will be calm and firm as I were Zeus.
I will descend to Hades and unloose
  My wife: prevail on pale Persephone,
Laving her love-locks with exalted dews

Of stern grey song; such roseate tunes espouse
That all the echoes of that lonely house
  Answer me sob for sob, that she decree
With love deep-seated in her lofty brows

Forth sparkling: and with Hades intercede,
So as I stir the judgment-seat, and plead,
  The awful brows may lighten, and decree
My wife's return -- a poet's lofty meed!

EXPLICIT LIBER SECUNDUS.

Aleister Crowley

LIBER TERTIUS VEL LABORIS

TO

THE MEMORY OF

IEHI AOUR,

WITH WHOM I WALKED THROUGH HELL, AND COMPELLED IT

"Neither were his hopes frustrated: For having appease them with them melodious sound of his voice and touch, prevailed at length so far, as that they granted him leave to take her away with him; but on this condition, that she should follow him, and he not to look back upon her, till he came to the light of the upper World; which he (impatient of, out of love and care, and thinking that he was in a manner past all danger) nevertheless violated, insomuch that the Covenant is broken, and she forthwith tumbles back again headlong into Hell." -- *The Wisdom of the Ancients.*

"Moody Pluto winks while Orpheus plays." -- *Rape of Lucrece.*

ORPHEUS TRAVELS TO HADES.

AS I pass in my flight
  On the awed storm cloud,
    Steeps steeper than sleep,
Depths deeper than night,
  I have furrowed and ploughed
    (Deep calling to deep!)
Through the spaces of light,
  The heads of them bowed
    For the fears that weep,
And the joys that smite,
  And the loves disallowed.
    They are risen; they leap;
They wing them in white,
  Crying aloud
    Words widowed that keep
The frost of their fires forgotten and faded from Memory's steep.

As I pass in my glory
  O'er sea and land,
    I smite the loud tune
From a fervid hand,
  By the promontory,
    The mountainous moon.
Vivid and hoary,
  Twin birds, as I hark
    Take fire, understand

Orpheus

The ways of the dark
  As an angel did guide me,
Waving the brand
  Of the dawn's red spark.
My measures mark
The influence fine
Of the voyage divine
Of the airy bark
Wherein I travel
O'er mountain and level,
  The land, and the sea.
And the beings of air,
  And the lives of the land,
And the daughters of fire,
  And the sons of the Ocean,
    Come unto me;
My chariot bear,
  My tunes understand,
My love desire,
  Share my emotion.
They gather, they gather,
Apollo, O father!
  They gather around;
  They echo the sound
Of the tune that rejoices,
  The manifold measure
Of feet tuned to voices
  Of terrible pleasure,
We pass in our courses
  Above the grey treasure
Of seas in Earth's forces,
  Her girdle, her splendour.
We bridle the horses
  Of sea as we lend her
  Tunes subtle and tender
To sink in her sources.
    The air's love? We rend her!
We pass to the West,
We sink on the breast
Of the Ocean to rest.

As I pass, as I madden
  In fury of flight,
The sea's billows gladden
  Invoking the light.
The depths of her sadden
  Not seeing the sight
Of the glorious one,
  Whose steed is the Sun,
  Whose journey is certain,
Who speeds to the gate,
  The visible curtain
Of visible fate.

My soul takes no hurt in
Their gloom: I await
The portals to rise
In the desolate skies.
I trust to my song
Irresistibly strong
 To sunder and shatter
 Those towers of matter.
They rise! Oh! They rise,
 The terrible towers
 Of Hades: they lift
Across the white skies
 Those terrible-cliffed
Rocks, where the hours
Beat vainly: where lies
 The horrible rift
 Of the earth's green bowers
 Where the wan ships drift,
 And the sun's rays shift,
And the river runs
 Whose banks have no flowers,
Whose waves have no suns.
 Sheer to the terror
Of heaven, the walls
 Strike; and the mirror
Of water recalls
 No truth, but dim error.
The soul of me falls
 Down to the glamour
Of dream; and fear
 Beats like a hammer.
Here! it is here!
 Lost are my friends;
The elements shrink
 Where the life-world ends
On the icy brink
 Of the sunless river;
 Ends, and for ever!

I pass to the portals
 Of death in my flight.
 I sound at the gates.
I call the immortals
 Of death and of night.
 I call on the Fates
By the summons of light.
 The gates are rended;
The rocks divide;
 My soul hath descended
Abreast of the tide.
 I, single and splendid,
 Death have defied!
I pass by the terrible gates and the guardians dragon-eyed.

Orpheus

I thunder adown
  The vast abyss.
(The journey's crown
  Is a woman's kiss!),
    What terrors to master!
    What fear and disaster
To gain the renown
  And the fadeless bliss!
I thunder aloud
  On the rocks as I fly,
Borne on a cloud
  In the gloomy sky.
Shaped like a shroud,
  Draped like a pall,
  I shrink not; I fall
To the blackness below
With my soul aglow.
  No taint of a fear!
For I know, I know
  Eurydice near,
  Eurydice here!
The purpose divine
  Thrills my soul as wine.
Now I pass to the soul of the dark, confronting the innermost shrine.

   Hail to ye, warders
   That guard the borders
    Of Hades! All hail to ye, dwellers of night!
   But I am the soul
   In a man's control.
    Ye have nought to do with the dweller of light!

   Hail to ye, hail
   In the hollow vale,
    Your weapons are lifted against me in vain.
   My lure shall charm ye,
   My voice disarm ye,
    For I am the soul overshadowed of pain!

   Hail to ye, wardens
   Of Death's grey gardens!
    O flowerless and vineless your bowerless vale!
   But I must alone
   To the wonderful throne.
    Let fall the vain spears, shadows! Hail to ye! Hail!

   The phantoms diminish,
   The shadows fall back.
    Lost in the vision
   In fires that finish
    Stark and black
     With lust and derision;

And all the illusion
  Is fallen to the ground.
    The warders are beaten
They go in confusion;
  Their place is not found.
    The air hath eaten
With wide-gaping jaws
  A furious folk.
Lost is the cause
  In Tartarean smoke.
I, through the wall
  Of impassable gloom,
    Apart from the sun,
Pass as a ghost,
  Bearing the lyre.
The sad notes fall
  To the sorrowful womb;
    One after one
They leap as a host
  With weapons of fire
On a desolate coast,
  Where love is lost
And the bitterness clings of fear, and the sadness gods of desire!

  Thrice girded with brass,
    Thrice bound with iron,
      The gate is in three
        Pillars of gold.
  But I will pass
    (My heart as a lion,
      My lyre as a key!)
        To the gates of old,
  To the place of despair
    And the walls of dread,
      The halls of the doomed,
    The homes of the dead,
  The houses where
    The beautiful air
      Is as air entombed.
  Nothing can shake
    Those terrible walls.
  No man can wake
    With silver calls
The home of the lost and the lone, the gate of the Stygian thralls.

  But thou, O Titan!
    O splendour triform!
    Gloomiest dweller
      Of uttermost night!
  My journey enlighten!
    O soul of the storm!
      Waker and queller
        Of sombre delight,

Orpheus

  Hecate! hearken
   The soul of my prayer!
  Glitter and darken
   Through sulphurous air!
Let the sacrifice move thee to joy, the invoker thy glory declare
   In words that shall please
   Thy terrible peace,
    O speedy to save,
In flames of fine fire that bedew the deepest Tatarean cave!

    [*Invoking HECATE*]

O triple form of darkness! Sombre splendour!
 Thou moon unseen of men! Thou huntress dread!
 Thou crowned demon of the crownless dead!
O breasts of blood, too bitter and too tender!
 Unseen of gentle spring,
 Let me the offering
 Bring to thy shrine's sepulchral glittering!
I slay the swart beast! I bestow the bloom
Sown in the dusk, and gathered in the gloom
 Under the waning moon,
  At midnight hardly lightening the East;
And the black lamb from the black ewe's dead womb
 I bring, and stir the slow infernal tune
  Fit for thy chosen priest.

Here where the band of Ocean breaks the road
 Black-trodden, deeply-stooping, to the abyss,
 I shall salute thee with the nameless kiss
Pronounced toward the uttermost abode
 Of thy supreme desire.
 I shall illume the fire
  Whence thy wild stryges shall obey the lyre,
Whence thy Lemurs shall gather and spring round,
Girdling me in the sad funereal ground
 With faces turned back,
  My face averted! I shall consummate
The awful act of worship, O renowned
 Fear upon earth, and fear in hell, and black
  Fear in the sky beyond Fate!

I hear the whining of thy wolves! I hear
 The howling of the hounds about thy form,
 Who comest in the terror of thy storm,
And night falls faster ere thine eyes appear
 Glittering through the mist.
 Of face of woman unkissed
  Save by the dead whose love is taken ere they wist!
Thee, thee I call! O dire one! O divine!
I, the sole mortal, seek thy deadly shrine,
 Pour the dark stream of blood,
  A sleepy and reluctant river

Aleister Crowley

Even as thou drawest, with thine eyes on mine,
  To me across the sense-bewildering flood
    That holds my soul for ever!

      The night falls back;
        The shadows give place;
        The threefold form
      Appears in the black,
        As a direful face
          Half seen in the storm.
      I worship, I praise
      The wonderful ways
      Where the smitten rays
        Of darkness sunder.
      The hand is lifted;
      The gates are rifted;
        The sound is as thunder!
      She comes to the summons,
      Her face as a woman's,
      Her feet as a Fear's,
      Turned back on her path
      For a sign of wrath: --
        She appears, she appears!
      I step to the river.
      The lyre-strings quiver;
      The limbs of me shudder;
        So cold is the mist;
          So dark is the stream;
            So fearful the boat;
      So horrid the rudder;
        So black is the tryst;
          So frightful the beam;
            So fearing to float;
      The steersman so dread,
The shadowy shape of a ghost that guides the bark of the dead!

      Aged and foul,
        His locks wreathe about him.
      Horrid his scowl!
        Haggard his soul!
        My songs control
      While they fear him and doubt him.
      I step in the boat,
        And the waters ache,
        And the old boards shake.
      I shall hardly float,
        So heavy the soul
          Of a living man
        On those waters that roll
        Nine times around
        The fatal ground;
Yet still to my singing we move on the river Tartarean.

Orpheus

So darker and colder
  The stream as we float:
    Blacker and bleaker,
      The mist on the river!
Stronger the shoulder
  Impels the sad boat.
    Sadder and weaker
      Shudder and quiver
The notes of the lyre.
Quenched is my fire
  In the fog of the air.
Dim my desire
  Cuts through the snare.
The cold confounds me;
The mist surrounds me;
  Life trembles and lowers;
Earth fades from my life.
The love of my wife,
  The light of the flowers,
  Earth's beautiful bowers.
Pass, and are not.
I am awed by the soul of the place, the hopeless, the desolate spot.

  Here is the wharf
    Wearily standing,
  Misshapen and dwarf,
    Well fit for such landing!
  Darker the bloom
    Of the night-flowers glows,
  Shadowing the tomb,
    The indicible woes.
    Dark and unlovely the cypress still grows
  Deformed and blistered,
    Stunted and blackened,
  Where the dead gleams glistered,
    The dusk-lights slackened.
  Such is the shore
    Who reacheth may never
    Return o'er the river!
  Here pace evermore
    The terrible ghosts
  Malignant of men,
    Whose airless hosts
      In wars unjust
  Went down to the den;
    Whose fury and lust
  Turned poison or steel
    On their own bad lives.
  Here whirls the grim wheel
    Where the dead soul strives
  Ever to climb
    To the iron nave,

Aleister Crowley

Find Space and Time,
  Or a God to save,
  Or a way o'er the wave.
The Fate contrives
That he never thrives.
  Revolving anon,
  The gleam is gone,
And the shadowy smile
Of Hecate darkens.
My sad soul hearkens;
  Moves fearfully on: --
O place of all places discrowned! Lamenting, I linger awhile!

  But fronting me tearful,
  Me full of lament,
  Shoots up the fearful
    Den of the hound.
  Ages they spent,
  Gods, in the graving
    That cavern profound,
  That temple of hate,
    Of horror and craving: --
  O who shall abate
    The moaning, the raving?
  Dark the dull flame
  Of the altar, the flood
  Of the black lamb's blood!
  But who shall proclaim
    That his soul can descry
The depth of that cavern immense where the guardian of Orcus may lie?

  Sleepest thou, devil?
  Monster of evil!
    Spawn of Typhon
    By Echidna's lust!
  The hateful revel
    In blood and dust!
  The obscene crone
  And the monster's terror!
  The hideous thrust
    Of an unclean thirst
  In the halls of error!
    Expunged and accurst,
  A lapping of hate,
    A bride-bed rotten,
  And thou, miscreate
    And misbegotten!

  O Hecate, hear me!
    The terrors awaken,
    The cavern is shaken
      With horrible groanings.
    Cryings and moanings

Orpheus

And howlings draw near me.
I tremble, I fear me!
  My lyre is forsaken.
The heart of the hollow
  Is helpless to bear
The notes of Apollo
  Through Stygian air.

But heavier shrieking
  Revolves and resounds
  In the ghastly profounds;
And the voice unspeaking
   Of the hound of the damned
  Runs eager, and bounds,
   Malignantly crammed
In my ears, and the noise
Of infernal joys
  In the houses of sin: --
Let me pass to a drier place, to the terrors unspoken within!

Dead silence succeeds
  The sound of the prayer.
   Again the loud lyre
Shudders and bleeds
  In the desolate air
   With a sound as of fire!
The hound recedes;
  But the gates stand there,
   Barring desire,
Barring the way
  Of the dead unburied,
   Unshrived, and unblessed;
They stand and pray
  In legions serried,
   Beating the breast,
  Tearing the hair,
   Rending the raiment.
  There is none to care.
   No golden payment
Availeth at all.
There is none to call;
  There is none to pity:
They stand in their pain
  At the gate of the city.
   There is none to feel
  Or give relief;
They are lost; they are vain;
  They are eaten of grief.
They are sore afraid,
  They are weary with care.
There is none to aid.
   There is none to pity.
   They wail in despair

At the gate of the city.

But I, shall I halt
  At the thrice-barred portal
In the lampless vault,
  I, half an immortal?
By love of my mother,
  By might of my lyre,
    By Nature's assistance,
I, I, not another
  Demand my desire,
    Rebuke your resistance,
By mighty Apollo
  Whose power yet abides,
Though his light may not follow
  Through Stygian tides!
By my power over things
  Both living and dead,
    By my influence splendid
    In heavenly court,
The song of me springs.
  My favour is dread.
    Be your portals rended!
    Your bolts be as nought!
The ethereal kings
  Encompass my head.
    My soul hath transcended
    The limits of thought!
Unbar me the gates!
  Revolve me the hinges!
Mine be the Fate!
  Mine be the springes
Wherein ye have taken
The spirits forsaken!
  But I, shall I quail at a nod?
  Shall I fail for a God?
Is the soul of me shaken?

Darklier winding
  And steeper the way,
Baffling and binding
  Eyes used to the day.
Rocks cloven by thunder
  And shattered by storm
Awry or asunder
  Rise and reform
In marvellous coils
  Round the adamant road
Whose tangles and toils
  Lead on the abode,
Where dwell in the light
  Of justice infernal
The judges that smite,

Orpheus

    That judge men aright,
      Whose laws are eternal!
    Those kings that in reigning
    For bribing or feigning
      Swerved never an hair
    From justice and truth;
      Turned never a care
    To wrath or to ruth;
      Did justice, and died.

    Thither I haste
      To face the austere
        Faces of peace.
          Shall the lyre cease?
    Its music be waste?
      Themselves not hear?
I stride to the presence and sing: and my soul is not conquered of fear.

Now the road widens and grows darker still
  As if the shadow of some ancient tower
Cast its deep spell on the reluctant will.

Still tortuous winds the deep descent; the hour
  Lies bitterer on my soul: I fear to fail,
To loose in vain the lyre's dissolving power

On the white souls armed in that triple mail
  Of justice, virtue, truth: percipience
Beyond the mute and melancholy veil

That covers from the drowsy eye of sense
  The subtle thought that hides behind the mask.
I fear indeed: but now the soul intense

Of truth precedes me and informs the task
  Of the steep ways: I gladden and go on
Ready to sing, to answer, or to ask

As all may happen: now the stern light shone
  Vivid across the blackness, and the rock
Recedes: the narrow stair is changed and gone

And the wide air invades: a mighty shock
  To my number senses void of vital air
And to my lure reverberate to mock

With changing echoes and discordant, where
  The dome reached up, almost to earth, so high
Rolled back the pillars and the walls, aglare

With iron justice' frightful symmetry
  Blazoned in blood-like flame, gushing from springs
Unseen, unguessed, incredible! There fly

The dreaded banners of the demon kings
  In fearful colours, and the vast inane
Dome catches music from my mouth, and rings

Back iron curses to the blessings vain
  I pour in desperate fervour from the lyre.
So, baffled by the echoes of hell's pain,

Blinded by grisly glamour of hell's fire,
  I take my refuge in the solitude
And grandeur of that irony of ire,

That mockery of mercy: thus I brood
  Apart, alone, upon the cause of Things
And wait those fearful Three. A lifeless mood

Stirs my grey being: ay! no passion springs
  In flowerless halls as these: awhile the mind
Wanders on void unprofitable wings

No whither: gains new strength at last to find
  Custom breed sight and hearing: in the hall
The sounds grow clear, the black fires fail to blind.

I see the mighty buttress of the wall
  Lost in its mighty measure: hear again
The lyre's low notes and light distinctly fall

A gentle influence in the place of pain.
  Oh now the central glory of the place
Falls splendid on the unbewildered brain,

And I am found contemplating a face
  More passionless than mortals': central sits
Throned on pure iron, with brass for carapace,

Minos: and either side of him befits
  The mighty Rhadamanthus throned on gold
And canopied with silver: sternly knits

His brows the awful Æacus, in cold
  Splendour of justice throned on carven lead;
And o'er his head twin dragons bend and hold

A cobra's hood made of some metal dread
  Impossible on earth: how calm, how keen
Flash their wise eyes, those judges of the dead,

In silent state: how eager, how serene
  Are the broad brows: the heart shrinks up and sinks,
Seeing no gallery to slip between

Orpheus

And pass those aged ones -- oft a man thinks
  He faces truth! I know this hour, alas!
That face to face with naked truth he shrinks.

His web of woven fiction may not pass
  (Though he believes it to be truth) with them
Who see his mind as though it were a glass

Without a shadow. Yet the ninefold gem
  And million-facet glory of my song
Glittering, made splendid in the diadem

Of flashing music shall assoil the wrong,
  A finer truth interpret. Though the heart
And core of music hold a poisonous throng

Of lies -- yet, sing it to sufficient Art,
  The lie abolishes itself -- the tune
Redeems the darkness -- the keen flashes start

Of truth availing though the midnight moon
  Darken, the stars be quenched in utter cloud,
And the high sun eclipsed at very noon.

So flash I back the glory calm and proud
  Irradiating the Three. So shall my lure
Sweep the vast courts with acclamation loud

Of splashing music, of exulting fire
  That revels in its penetrating cover
Of azure life that smites its flickering spire

Of sworded splendour inwards, to discover
  Not justice, not discernment, not desire,
Not passion, but the sheer will of a lover!

                    MINOS.
Substantial, stern, and strong,
Who lifts an alien lyre?
Confounds our echoes dire
With strange and stubborn song?

                    ÆACUS.
Here in the House of Dole
Where shadows hardly dare
Stand, who doth deem to fare
Forth from the outer air
Mortal, a strenuous soul?

                RHADAMANTHUS.
The large and lordly land
Fertile of earth hath sent
With dolorous intent

Some shape or element.
What spell of might hath rent
The veil of Hell, and bent
Death's purpose to his hand?

MINOS.
What shaft from the bow of Apollo?

ÆACUS.
What quiver of wonder
Hath cleft the black walls of the hollow

RHADAMANTHUS.
What terror?

MINOS.
What thunder
Hath shaken Hell's gates to the base?

ÆACUS.
Withstanding the guards to their face?

RHADAMANTHUS.
Hath rent him asunder
The portals of Dis in his wrath?

MINOS.
Hath made for his will
An arrow of light for his path?

ÆACUS.
Left stagnant and chill
The waters of Styx unappeased?
The keys of our prison hath he seized.

RHADAMANTHUS.
A mortal!

MINOS.
An ill
Most alien to Heaven, by Zeus!

ÆACUS.
But impiety's doom,
By Poseidon, shall fill for his use
No well-omened tomb.

RHADAMANTHUS.
By Hades, our dogs let us loose!
Let death in the gloom

Bring peace to the Hall of the dead!

                MINOS.

  A passionate being!
No weal to the light of his head
  In the place of the seeing!

                ÆACUS.

Awake, wild justice of dread!
   Lest shadows be fleeing
In fear of the portent to lurk
   In a deeper-detested
Cave, ere we wake to the work.

              RHADAMANTHUS.

  Black snakes many-crested,
Arise! lest the calm of the murk
  From our places be wrested.

                MINOS.

Who art thou?

                ÆACUS.

    What ails thee to irk
  From earth tender-breasted
To the milkless dugs of the grave
  And the iron breasts of the pit?

              RHADAMANTHUS.

Can a bodily presence save
  Against a shadowy wit?

                MINOS.

Thy hope doth dwell, O slave,
  Where thy mother fashioned it,
Oh heart of a fool, in thy breast.

                ÆACUS.

  Away, away to the skies!

              RHADAMANTHUS.
That our dead may take their rest.

                MINOS.

  Arise to the air, arise!

                ÆACUS.

Away to the mountain crest!

              RHADAMANTHUS.
  Veil, veil from the awful eyes!

MINOS.

Endure thy heart as it may,
   And steel thine heart,
Thou shalt hear and know and obey
   As I say "Depart";
Lest the arrow find its way
   And the sternly-shapen dart.

ÆACUS.

A second our justice waits.

RHADAMANTHUS.

It falleth anon.

MINOS.

O fool of hopes and hates
   Arise and begone!

ÆACUS.

O toy of the mirthless fates!
   Who art thou to con
The mysteries of the dead in the back-souled bastion?

MINOS, ÆACUS, RHADAMANTHUS.

Away! away! to the light of day!
   Now as it may: then as it must.
We are loath to pardon, and loath to slay,
   Void of greed and anger and lust, --
But we are iron and thou art clay;
   We are marble and thou but dust.

ORPHEUS.

O iron, bow to silver's piercing note!
O marble, see the shape of ivory!
My justice fountains from a sweeter throat;
   My death is bound beyond eternity.

O wise and just, hear ye the voice of man,
   Not seeking to involve in woven spells
Or trickery the decree Tartarean,
   By words to blink that justice which is Hell's!

I came indeed before this awful throne
   To seek a party favour, but I wait
Shuddering and silent, steadfast and alone,
   And change my music at the call of Fate.

For while ye spake in tumult, in this ear
   A music rang from earth's remotest mine,
From star and comet, flaming wheel and sphere,
   From Hell's deep vault and from the House divine.

Orpheus

A voice diverse, a voice identical
  Called me this hour from bitterest woes and black,
Constraining eloquence and mighty thrall
  Of cosmic agony, and wrung me back

From my poor plea to challenge in my song
  The whole domain of deeply-seated law,
Launch thunders not Olympic at the strong
  Bars of the Order backed with strength and awe

That men call Will of Zeus: the after scheme
  And primal fate and most primordal plan
Shaped from the earth's first protoplasmic dream
  Up to the last great mischief that is man.

All this I challenge: that the suns and stars
  Work in due order and procession meet
Without caprice in viewless, changeless bars,
  Nor self-determinate in their wingless feet.

All nature and all consciousness and thought
  He hath thrown asunder and divided them;
Fixing a gulf of agony athwart,
  Where rolls a tide no soul of man may stem.

Himself fixed high, he mocked us with his name
  Of "reconciler," and of "one beyond all";
And cast his shadow to the deep, to shame
  That oneness in its own division's thrall;

So that Himself appears in cloud and fire
  Distorted in the world's distorted mirror;
And dark convulsion and confusion dire
  Stands for his form of error and of terror.

But I perceive, I Orpheus, Lord of Song,
  And every Lord of Song that me shall follow
Down steeps of time's own agony and wrong,
  Shall see the lightning bridge the dreadful hollow

With jagged flame of master-music, hear
  The blind curse thunder forth against in vain
When the swift glory of the rolling sphere
  Of song pours forth its utterance, keen with pain,

Mad with delight, and calm beyond woe and pleasure.
  Yea, every son of this my soul shall know
In the swift concourse of his music's measure
  One thing impatient of this to and fro

March of hell's dancers. I perceive a key
  To lock the prison of the world on him

That built the iron walls and made decree
Long past in aeons now grown gray and dim,

Like halls ancestral whence their folk have fled,
 The marbles all are broken, and the weeds
Grown o'er the bones of the unquiet dead,
 And time's remorse avails not on its deeds.

I see that time is one: future and past
 Are but one present; space is one, the North
And South and all the sixfold shame holds fast
 No more: the poet's fiat hath gone forth

And tamed the masters of division. Me
 Nor sun can burn, nor moon make mad, nor time
Alter: I drown not in the deepest sea,
 Nor choke where icy mountain ridges climb

The steeps of heaven; but these, these children, cry
 Their bitter cry for justice. Mighty Ones,
Lords of the Dusk, incline ye, mercifully,
 Rightly, to misery of all stars and suns

And planets and all grains of dust that sorrow --
 Hark! from grim Tartarus, most doleful bound,
Their throats of anguish notes of triumph borrow
 At my loud strain's unprofitable sound.

For who are ye? Poor judges of the dead,
 In your stern eyes the sadness is mine own,
Mingled with sense that all your forces dread
 Are vain to take the spirit from one stone.

I would have called to ye in wild strong joy;
 "Arise, O Lords of Justice, and be girt
With lightnings, and be ardent to destroy
 This Fool's creation and to heal its hurt

With swift annihilation!" Ye are vain,
 Alas! poor powers! But yet the damned rejoice
Hearing the splendour, prophet in my strain,
 And certain comfort in my mighty voice.

For this shall be, that in the utter end
 Shall be an end, that in the vast of time
Shall come a ceasing, and the steel bar bend
 Of the God's will, himself from his sublime

Pinnacled house in heaven headlong cast
 Like his own thunder to the abyss of nought
When space and time and being shall be past,
 And the grim thinker perish with his thought.

Orpheus

Therefore I leave in hands unshakable
 The destinies of being, and care not
For all the miseries of the damned in hell,
 Or the vain gods' unenviable lot.

I leave the cry of chaos, and recall
 My private pang and woe particular,
One drop of water by mischance let fall
 From some white slave's divinely carven jar.

O Lords of justice, universal woe
 Hath yet its shadows in a singer's soul,
He feels the arrow from a party bow
 Who yet hath strength to struggle with the whole.

I love my wife. The many-coloured throne
 Of Grecian meadows hath nor charm nor lure
Now she is gone. Lamenting and alone
 My dulled heart aches, most that it must endure.

Give this decree, O masters! Few the days
 And light the hours since Heracles descended
The dusky steep, the intolerable ways,
 And one prey -- Theseus -- from your prisons rended

By might of godhead and the skill of man.
 But now with music from a Muse's breast
Sweetened with milk of tenderness, I scan
 Your eyes with hope, and with a man's unrest

And a man's purpose I appeal. Be just,
 O ye whom greater justice baulks and bars!
Return my lover from the unkind dust
 To the sweet light of the eternal stars!

Be kind, and from the unjust place of fear
 Return by kindness her, the innocent one,
From the grey places to the waters clear
 And meadows fair, and light of moon and sun!

Relent. Reverse the doom. I see your eyes
 Quiver despite ye: but your hands ye wring;
Little by little bitter tears arise
 Like stubborn water from a frozen spring,

And deep unrest is seated in your limbs.
 Ye pitty me. Ye pity. Mute and weak
With the long trouble of persistent hymns
 I bow myself and listen while ye speak.

MINOS.

 Brethern, what need of wonder
 That Hell is burst asunder

Shaken from base to brow, as if with Zeus' own thunder?
  What wonder if our peace
  Broke, and our mysteries
Quaked at the presence of these solemnities?

ÆACUS.

  Child of the earth and heaven,
  Our spirits thou hast riven
With words we must admit, with power of song – whence given?
  Neither of God nor man,
  Thy song's amazing span
Hath caused strange joy among the woes Tartarean.

RHADAMANTHUS.

  Never in the centuries
  Till godlike Heracles
Burst the wild bonds, hath mortal found the fatal knees;
  Nor hath the bitter cry
  Of worlds in agony
Answered the groans of those who weep, and cannot die.

MINOS.

  Iron of heart and strong,
  We also suffer wrong.
We know these words are just. We avail not. Though thy song
  Were the sole word of Zeus,
  Should that avail to loose
The bands of Being firm, invulnerable dews
  Tincturing its bitter brass,
  Shielding its vital mass
From every word that cries, "Thus, and thy day shall pass."

ÆACUS.

  Typhon! Typhon! Typhon!
  Heard ye that awful moan
Leap through the blackness from the miserable throne?
  Vain as each pallid ghost,
  Where is thy fatal boast,
Destroyer named of old on Khem's disastrous coast?
  Old power of evil curled
  Below the phantom world,
Canst thou destroy, whose might to misery is hurled?

RHADAMANTHUS.

  What god beyond these twain
  Abides or may remain
Seated, too strong to quell, exalted over pain?
  Aloof from time and chance,
  Fate, will and circumstance,
Canst thou not wither Life with one indignant glance?
  Thy name we know not; Thine
  Is the unbuilded shrine.

Orpheus

We doubt us if Thou be among the powers divine!

MINOS.

Bound by strict line and law,
Fearful with might and awe,
We hold the powerless power
For many an aged hour.
We move not from our place.
We ask nor give not grace,
Nor change our lordly looks before a suppliant's face.

ÆACUS.

Stern in all justice, we
Assent aloud to thee,
We affirm thy cause as right:
We put forth all the might
Of aid: and all is done.
Out utmost power is none
To lift one soul to live and look upon the sun.

RHADAMANTHUS.

For righteous thought and deed
Apportioning its meed;
For evil act and mind
Rewarding in its kind;
So sit we: but our power
Apportions not an hour
To light the dying lamp, revive the faded flower.

MINOS.

Be thou, be strong to sing!

ÆACUS.

Loose arrows from the string!

RHADAMANTHUS.

Bid the wild word take wing!

MINOS.

Hades hath evil fame
To suppliants -- bitter shame! --
Inexorable.

ÆACUS.
                        Aim

Yet the swift prayer, abide
His word whate'er betide.
What worse?

RHADAMANTHUS.

    The Gods thy guide!
Go and assail him!

Aleister Crowley

                    MINOS.
                          Stay,
The Queen of Hell!

                    ÆACUS.
                        That way
Leads to the light of day.

                RHADAMANTHUS.
A woman's heart may yearn,
To a man's love may turn.

                    MINOS.
Should she, the ravished, spurn
A man whose love is reft?

                    ÆACUS.
Meadows and flower, she left
To Him -- O bosom cleft
With a wife's loss! -- a wife.

                RHADAMANTHUS.
Too doubtful is the strife.

                    MINOS.
Yet go! perchance to life.

                    ÆACUS.
Go! and the Gods above
Guard thee, O soul of love!

                RHADAMANTHUS.
I doubt me much thereof.

                    ORPHEUS.
Ah me! I find ye but ill counsellors.
For I will conquer. Have I spent these stores
Of will and song for nought? Hell's heart may rend,
But mine endureth even to the end.

Severe and righteous Lords, O fare ye well!
Are not my feet forced forward on a road
Leading to innermost abodes of Hell

Exalted as above the green abode
Of nymphs on broad Olympus, raises high
Its head the kingly snow, gigantic load

Of sombre whiteness cleaving through the sky

Orpheus

For gods to dwell in? So I pass the hall
And seek the gloomy thrones of majesty,

Where I may pledge my last despairing call
Unto the mightiest of the House of Dread,
And loosen Death's inexorable thrall

And bring my lover from among the dead.
Now in the blackness of the rocks that span
The dolorous way I spy a golden thread

Veined in the strength of the obsidian
Flowing and growing, joining vein to vein,
Like fresh blood in the arteries of man,

Up to the very heart. And as I go
Loosen the knees of anguish and grow dim
The shattering flames of pain: the songs of woe

Flicker and alter to a solemn hymn
Chanted in slowest measure in deep awe.
Now as a yew-tree sends a mighty limb

Shooting to sunset, the black road's black maw
Gapes to the westward; the great trunk divides
And all the armies of infernal law

Stand ranked about the venerable sides
Of the black cave: they speak not; dumb they stand
And all the frost of all the air abides

Upon them, as a vampire stooped and spanned
The white throat of a maiden and held still
Her powers by virtue of its hate's command,

Somewhat like love's: so all the solemn chill
Invades those statued ranks of warriors,
And I pass through, the lightning of my will

A steady stream of flame: high instinct pours
Its limpid light of water on my mind,
So that I range inhospitable shores

Assured of Her I shall most surely find
Ere the end be: awake, O living lyre,
Since in the narrow way and pass confined

I see a darkness infinite as fire,
Clear as all spirit vision, lustrous yet
As ebony shows in caverns rendered dire

By dreadful magic, or as if pure jet
Had taken of itself an inner light,

And its own blackness filled night's coronet

With a new jewel: so I see aright
Where no light is like earth's. The path grows broad
And lofty, till the whole hall springs to sight,

And I am standing where the dreaded Lord
And Lady of the region of the lost
Hold awful sway: yet here the flaming sword

Of sight is broken by the deadly frost
That clusters round their thrones: a mist of fire
Congealed to vital darkness: yet exhaust

Like a seer's magic glass of air: expire
The dumb black hours in fear: but I am ware,
Well ware, by instinct surer still and higher

Than the own sight of soul that they are there,
No mockery of their presence: so even hither
My mother's might is on me, on I flare

Into wild war of song: my keen notes wither
The flowers of frost about me and I turn
Ever the strength and mastering frenzy thither

With energy of madness: yea, I burn!
My soul burns up upon the lyre! I lend
My whole life's vigour to one song, to earn

Their guerdon of the gods, a god to friend,
And seek through devious ways a single end.

[*Invoking* HADES.

Str. 1.

Now is the gold gone of the year, and gone
  The glory of the world, and gathered close
  The silver of the frost. Far splendid snows
Shine where the bright anemone once shone.
  Ay! for the laughter live
  Of youths and maids that strive
In amorous play, the ancient saws of eld
  And wisdom mystical
  From bearded lips must fall,
Old eyes behold what young eyes ne'er beheld:
Namely, the things beyond the triple veil
  Of space and time and cause, eternal woof
  Of misery overproof:
And aged thoughts assail
  The younger hopes, and passion stands aloof,
And silence takes possession, and the tale

Of earth is told and done.
Then from the Sire of all the Gods, from War
And Love and Wisdom and the eternal Sun
Worship is torn afar:
  While unto Thee, O Hades, turn we now,
  Awful of breast and brow,
And hear thee in the sea, behold thee in the Star.

Ant. 1 [*Echo of the Damned*].

Ay! is the earth and upper ether gone,
  And all the joy of earth, and gathered close
  The darkness and the death-wind and the snows
On us on whom the sun of air once shone.
  What souls are left alive
  Vainly lament and strive,
For they shall join the dead of utmost eld;
  The concourse mystical
  Who see the seasons fall
Shall soon behold what all we have beheld: --
The accursed stream, the intolerable veil
  Of night and death and hell, disastrous woof
  Of anguish overproof
That fruitless wills assail
  Ever in vain: good fortune stands aloof
And all kind gods: we, taking up the tale
  Of dead men past and done,
Declare that ceaseless is the eternal war,
  And victory stedfast set against the Sun.
Yet we perceive afar
  Even in Hades, at the end, not now,
  Some light upon his brow,
Some comfort in the sea, some refuge in the Star.

Str. 2.

O thou! because thy chariot is golden,
  And beautiful thy coursers, and their manes
  Flecked with such foam as once upon the sea
Bore Aphrodite, and thy face is olden,
  Worn with dim thought and unsuspected pains,
  And all thy soul fulfilled of majesty;
Because the silence of thy house is great,
And thy word second spoken after Fate,
And thy light stricken of thine own grim hand;
Because thy whisper exceedeth the command
Of Zeus; thy dim light far outshines his glory;
  Because, as He the first is, Thou the last: --
  Therefore I take up sorrow in my hands,
And ply thine ear with my most doleful story,
  Asking a future, who have lost a past:
  A guerdon of my singing like the land's
When spring breaks forth from winter, and the blood
Of the old earth laughs in every new-born bud.

Ant. 2 [*Echo of the Damned*].

O thou! because thy lyre is keen and golden
  And beautiful thy numbers through our veins
    Pouring delight, as on the starry sea
Burn gems of rapture; though the houses olden
  Relax awhile their unredeeming pains,
    And through dead slaves thrill bounteous majesty?
Though the strong music of thy soul be great: --
Shall thy desire avail to alter Fate?
Or impious hands unloose the awful hand?
Or futile words reverse the great command?
Or what availeth? Though great Hades' glory
  Stoop to thy prayer, and answer thee at last,
    Should Clotho catch the thread in weaving hands,
Respin what Atropos once cut -- that story
  Were vain for thee -- that which is past is past,
    Nor can Omnipotence avail the land's
Death -- Spring's is alien through ancestral blood,
And a new birth is current in the bud.

Str. 3.

Think, then, the deed impossible is done
  Since Theseus fared forth to the ambient air!
His thread once cut -- was that indeed respun
  Or patched by witchery? a deceit? a snare?
I tell ye; past and future are but one,
  And present -- nothing; shall not Hades dare
His own omnipotence against the Sun,
  And let no tittle of his glory share
With all the earth's recuperating wheel,
And every dawn's sure falchion-flash of steel?

Ant. 3. [*Echo of the Damned*].

Indeed, a deed impossible was done
  Were the new Theseus heavier than the air.
Nay! but a new thread phantom-frail was spun
  And men's blind eyes discovered not the snare,
Else were that elder cord and this yet one,
  Cut but in fancy. Yet, shall mortal dare
To fling a wanton word against the Sun,
  And stand forth candidate for lot and share
Where hangs Prometheus, rolls Ixion's wheel,
And the stone rolls upon the limbs of steel?

Epode.

These echoes, in my mind foul torturers,
  Present my fears, and image my distrust.
No answer comes, no voice the silence stirs
  With joyful "may" or melancholy "must."

Nor, though the gloom requicken, may I see
  Hades enthroned, my prayers who heedeth nought,
Nor glowing tear of bowed Persephone
  Drooped earthward for the ninefold misery wrought.
In utter sorrow ever bound she stays,
  Hears not my song, nor heedeth anything,
Whose mind lamenting turns to ancient days
  And Nysian meadows and the hour of spring.
Yea, but perchance to touch that secret chord
  Were to awake that sorrow into life;
Sting, as a wound a deep-envenomed sword,
  The inmost soul of the Aidonean wife.
Listen! I tune my music to that hour;
  The careless maidens and the virgin laughter,
The bloom of springtide and the fatal flower,
  And all that joy the sorrow echoing after.
So that, dread Hades, thou mayst hear and yield,
  Thyself unmastered and inexorable,
The gentle maid as crying in that field,
  Now thy soul's keeper on the throne of Hell!
Hail, Hades! Thou who hearest not my song,
  Repealest not the heaven's unjust decree,
Revengest not for me the woe and wrong,
  Shalt glean my sorrow from Persephone.
Hail, Hades! In the gloom the echoing cry
  Swells, and the chorus darkens as I sing,
And all the fibres of Eternity
  Shake as I loose the loud indignant string.
Hail, Hades! hear thy wrong proclaimed aloud,
  And thou the wronger safe because too great.
To like offence harden thy neck, and proud
  Blow thou the dismal challenge unto Fate!

In Asia, on the Nysian plains, she played,
  A slender maid,
With the deep-bosomed Oceanides;
  Where the tall trees
Girded the meadow with grave walls of green.
  Alone, unseen,
The tender little lady strayed,
  Moving across the breeze.
It was a meadow of soft grass and flowers,
  Where the sweet hours
Lingered and laughed awhile ere noon reposes.
  There were red roses
And crocus, and flag-flowers, and violets,
  And hyacinth, regrets
Of the ill-fortuned God, the quoit-player;
  And soft cool air
Stirred all the field -- and there were jessamines
  And snaky columbines.
So all these maidens played, and gathered them
  From sad green stem

Rejoicing blooms with sunlight mixed therein.
  But she, for sin
And iron heart of the ill-minded Zeus,
  Caught up the dews
Deep on her ankles, and went noiselessly
  Toward the laughing sea,
And sought new blossoms -- O the traitor, Earth,
  That brought to birth
That day, as favouring the desire that swelled
  Beneath her heart of eld,
Where dwelt the lonely, the detested one
  Intolerant of the sun,
Hades! But Earth for love of him, for spite
  Of the young girl's delight,
And shame of her own age, brought forth that hour
  The fatal flower,
Narcissus -- which what soul of man shall smell
  Goes down to hell,
Caught in the scent of sin -- for such a doom
  Demeter's flying loom
Hath woven for revenge and punishment.
  The bright child went
Thither; an hundred heads of blossom sprang;
  The green earth sang,
And the skies laughed, and danced the sea's young feet
  For joy of it.
So the child went across that fairest plain
  To pluck, to strain
That blossom of all blossoms to her heart,
  Her long hands dart,
Exceeding delicate and fair, to cull
  That bloom too beautiful,
Eager to gather the fresh floral birth.
  The grim black earth
Gaped; roared athwart the gulf the golden car;
  And flaming far
The four white horses with their flashing manes!
  The might-resisting reins
Lay in the ghastly hands, the arms of fear
  Of that dread charioteer,
Death; and great Hades armed stood glittering,
  Stooped to his spring,
And whirled the child to the beneath abode.
  O heavy load!
O bitter harvest of rich-rolling tears!
  What cry who hears?
A shrill shrill cry to father Zeus cried she,
  Forlorn Persephone!
Heard was that agony of grief by none
  Save only by the Sun,
And Her who sat within her awful cave,
  Contemplative and grave,
Hecate, veiled with a shining veil

Utterly frail
As the strange web of dainty thoughts she wove,
   Somewhat like love.
She heard, and great Apollo: neither stayed
   Hades, nor stretched to aid
A pitying hand. O pitiful! O grief
   Baffling belief!
The gentle child -- the cruel god -- Ah me!
   Persephone!
Thus of thy grace, thy sorrow, thy young way
   Torn from the day
Of all thy memory of soft shining flowers
   And happy-hearted hours,
Mayst thou be very pitiful to me
   Who aye have pitied thee,
     Persephone!

PERSEPHONE.

Ah me! I feel a stirring in my blood.
Pours through my veins a delicate pale flood
Of memory. Not the pale and terrible
Goddess whose throne is manifest in Hell
-- I am again a child, a playful child.

ORPHEUS.

And therefore, O most beautiful and mild
Sweet mother! art the girl beloved again
Of Hades mighty on the Nysian plain.
And therefore are thine eyes with sorrow dim
For me, and thy word powerful with him.

PERSEPHONE.

   Ah me! no fruit for guerdon,
   Who bore the blossom's burden;
There shines no sunlight toward Persephone.
   Ravished, O iron-eyed!
   From my young sisters' side,
Torn and dragged down below the sundered sea,
   No joy is mine in all thy bed,
   And all thy sorrow shaken on my head.

   Cursed above gods be thou
   Whose blind unruffled brow
Rules the grim place of unsubstantial things!
   Hated, to me thy face
   Turns not the glance of grace.
I rule unloved above the infernal kings,
   And only thee in all deep Hell
   I charm in vain, despair my royal spell.

By might of famine long
And supplication strong
Demeter won the swift Hermetic word:
   In bitter days of eld
   Thus by great force compelled
The glad earth saw me, careless of my lord,
   Rise to her crystal streams and sapphire seas,
   And Theseus thus owed life to Heracles.

Thou mockest me with power;
   Thy sceptre's awful dower
Avails me nothing. Shall a mortal bring
   Such pity wrapped in song
   And Echo's choral throng
Of all things live and dead to hear me sing; --
   And I by pity moved and love
   Have not thy voice to grant him grace thereof?

Inexorable Lord!
   Accursed and abhorred
Of men, begin in Hell to show thy grace!
   Not to a man's weak life,
   Not to thy shuddering wife,
But to the queen's unfathomable face
   Dread beyond sorcery and prayer,
   And fearful even because it is so fair!

Yea, from the ghastly throne
   Unchallenged and unknown
Let the fierce accents roll athwart the skies!
   My voice is given, my power
   Fares forth to save the flower
Broken but plucked not by these fingers wise.
   I love the song -- be thou not mute,
   But turn a lucky lot towards the suit!

ORPHEUS.

   In vain, O thou veiled
     Immutable queen!
   Thy strong voice bewailed,
     Thy fair face was seen!
   It flushed up and paled;
     The song echoed clean --
But alas! for the veil of the night and the fear that is ever between!

   Of pity unfilled
     And void of remorse,
   He moves unappealed
     In the terrible course.
   But the lyre is unchilled: --
     By force unto force
He shall answer me power unto power at the source of its source!

Orpheus

    Dost thou hear how the weight
      Of the earth and the moon
    Shudder, as if fate
      Were involved in the tune?
    The portals of hate
      Shake at the rune
Of the magical nature-cry, the song from the mountains hewn!

    To the horrible hollow
      In Tartarus steep,
    O song of me, follow!
      I flee to the deep.
    That word of Apollo
      Shall shudder and leap;
That word in the uttermost night shall awake them who know not of sleep.

    Hear, O ye Three,
      In the innermost pit
    Dwellers that be!
      Tartarus, split!
    Arise unto me
      For I call ye with wit
Of the words that constrain and compel, of the summons ordered and fit!

    O daughter of Earth,
      Tisiphone dread,
    The ophidian girth,
      And the blood-dripping head,
    In hideous mirth
      Bring living and dead
To torture! Arise! I conjure by the might of the words I have said.

    Megæra, thou terror,
      O daughter of Night
    Whose sight in a mirror
      Is death of affright,
    Winged with error,
      I chain thee, and cite
The words that thy soul must obey if a mortal but say them aright!

    Alecto! I call thee,
      My words ring thee round.
    My spells enwall thee.
      My lure is crowned
    With might to appal thee
      With terror profound.
Arise! O Alecto, arise! for my song hath compelled thee and bound.

    Ye furies of Hell!
      Ye terrors in Heaven!
    The strength of the spell
      Is as thunder at even

Aleister Crowley

    The rocks of the fell
      That hath blasted and riven
Come forth! I invoke ye, Erinyes, the charm of the One that is seven.

    By the Five that are One,
      And the One that is Ten;
    By the snake in the sun
      And her mirror in men;
    By the four that run
      And return them again;
By the fire that is lit in the Lion, the wave in the Scorpion den!

    By the One that is Seven,
      The whirling eyes;
    The Two made Eleven,
      The dragon's devise;
    The Eight against Heaven,
      All crowns of lies;
Come forth! I invoke ye, Erinyes, move, answer, take shapes and arise!

    By the cross and the wheel
      I call ye to hear;
    By the dagger of steel
      I command ye, give ear!
    By the word that ye feel,
      The summons of Fear;
Come forth! I invoke ye, Erinyes, move, answer, arise and appear!

    For my purpose is swift,
      And my vengeance strong;
    I shall not shift;
      I shall cry the wrong.
    My voice I uplift
      In terrible song
As your forms take shape before me in the likeness for which ye long.

    The shape of my passion
      And bitter distress
    Shall clothe ye, and fashion
      An equal dress.
    Ye shall force compassion
      With awful stress
From the soul that hat mocked me, and turned his heart from my song's excess.

    The ruler of Hell,
      The invisible Lord,
    Hath laughed at my spell,
      Hath slept at my word.
    He hath heard me well --
      Awake, O Sword!
Shall he flout a suppliant thus and no answer of favour accord?

    If mercy be sundered

Orpheus

    From splendour and power;
  If he answer with thunder
    The plaint of a flower;
  Shall justice wonder
    If Furies devour
So bitter a heart, set a term to his date that was aye but an hour?

  Avenge me, ye forces
    Of horror and wrath!
  Clear the dread courses!
    Split open the path!
  With cruel remorse is
    His heart brought to scath.
And a terror is on him at last, the seed of his hate's aftermath.

                  MEGÆRA.
Ha! who invokes? What horror rages
  Here, to compel our murderous hands to smite?

                  ALECTO.
What mortal summons? Who his battle wages
  So strongly as to call the seed of Night?

                  TISIPHONE.
Ha! The grim tyrant of despair engages
  Our deadly anguish with his useless might.

                  HADES.
Detested fiends! avaunt!

                  MEGÆRA.
                                      He speaks!

                  ALECTO.
                                                  He thunders!

                  TISIPHONE.
His lightnings split the living rock.

                  MEGÆRA.
                                      Hell sunders
The livid walls and iron-bound prisons of death.

                  HADES.
Thus! to your towers and wail!

                  ALECTO.
                  He speaks!

                  TISIPHONE.
                                        His breath

Is cold as ours.

HADES.
Depart! Due silence keep,
Lest I enchain ye in a fouler deep
Than aught your horror pictures!

MEGÆRA.
Dost thou hear,
Sister?

ALECTO.
Sweet sister!

TISIPHONE.
Dost thou think we fear
Who are all fear? or feel, who are but pain?

MEGÆRA.
Creep round his heart, and cluster in his brain,
Ye serpents of my hair!

ALECTO.
His blood shall drip
For sweet warm juice on my decaying lip.

TISIPHONE.
My fearful wings enfold him!

ALECTO.
My foul eyes
Hold his in terror!

MEGÆRA.
All my agonies
Crawl in his vitals!

TISIPHONE.
He is mine, mine, mine!
Pour forth of Thebes' abominable wine!
Mine, O thou god, detested and adored!

MEGÆRA.
Mine! he is mine! my lover and my lord!

ALECTO.
Mine! I am in his shape!

MEGAERA.
Despair! Dispute
Never my passion!

Orpheus

TISIPHONE.
Sisters! Be ye mute!

I am the livid agony that starts
Damp on his brow; the horror in his heart's
Envenomed arteries! and I the fear,
The torment, and the hate!

MEGÆRA.
Be of good cheer!

Rend him apart! Hunger and lust we sate,
Equal in terror on that heart of hate.

ALECTO.
Hell's throne be kingless!

TISIPHONE.
Mortal! is it well,

Our vengeance on the impious lord of Hell!

ORPHEUS.
Well! it is well! And yet my eyes are wet
To see such anguish.

MEGÆRA.
Tear the fatal net!

ALECTO.
Bite with strong acid his congealing blood!

TISIPHONE.
Rend out the bowels!

MEGÆRA.
    Pour the monstrous flood
Of unclean wisdom in his soul!

PERSEPHONE.
Desist!

ALECTO.
O face of woman wretched and unkissed,
What hast thou here to do with us?

TISIPHONE.
Be quiet!

MEGÆRA.
Quench not the fire of murder!

ALECTO.
Loose the riot

Of worms beneath the skull!

TISIPHONE.
                                                          Tear wide apart
The jaws!

MEGÆRA.
                    Force fear against the inmost heart!

PERSEPHONE.
Mercy! I plead, sweet sisters!

ORPHEUS.
                                                          And I plead
Vengeance, and help in my extremest need
Pile up the torture! Had he not the power,
And silence mocked me?

MEGÆRA.
                                            Urge us hour by hour,
Thou couldst not add one particle of pain.

ALECTO.
He speaks not! Bid his torture speak again!

TISIPHONE.
Speak, murderer!

MEGÆRA.
                          Hades! answer us!

ALECTO.
                                                           Expel
These torments from thy being, us from Hell,
Or Zeus from Heaven!

TISIPHONE.
Or else obey!

MEGÆRA.
                                                              Obey!

ALECTO.
Obey!

HADES.
O throne of hell! O night! O day
Of anguish exquisite beyond control,
Fibre and substance of my inmost soul!

Orpheus

There is a power not mine, and yet in me
Burning its cold and cruel agony
With icy flames, its cutting poison fangs
Striking my being with detested pangs.
Alas! of me and not to be expelled,
Conjured, assuaged, averted. Grey as eld
The juice of blood that stagnates in my veins
Appals their current with avenging pains: --
O pain! O pitiful and hateful sense
Of agony and grief and impotence!
O misery of the day when Orpheus bore
First his loud lyre across the Stygian shore!
Hath Hell no warders? Is the threefold gate
Brazen in vain against the foot of Fate?
Now is but little choice -- abase my pride,
Or sink for ever to the gloomy tide
Of fire beneath the utmost reach and span
Of Stygian deeps and walls Tartarean.
Yet I abide.

MEGÆRA.
Fall! Fall!

ALECTO.
Descend the abyss!

TISIPHONE.
Link the lewd fiend with your incestuous kiss!

MEGÆRA.
Hither!

ALECTO.
O hither!

HADES.
Steams a newer shape
Of threefold terror.

TISIPHONE.
Shall the god escape
The monstrous wedlock?

ALECTO.
Let him turn again
His horrid passion to the Nysian plain!

MEGÆRA.
Echidna!

ALECTO.
Mother of the Sphinx and snake
Of Colchus, and the marsh-beast of the lake
Lernean, of Chimaera and Hell's hound --

TISIPHONE.
Answer!

ALECTO.
    Arise!

MEGÆRA.
                Awake from the profound!

TISIPHONE.
Here is a worthy partner unto thee
To wake thy womb with monstrous progeny,
Yet more detested and detestable
Than all the shapeless brood of hate and Hell.

ECHIDNA.
Ha! rose-lipped lover! Welcome to this bed!

MEGÆRA.
She plays with words of love!

ALECTO.
            Her black eyes shed
Disease for tears.

TISIPHONE.
            Her fangs and lips are red
With gouts of putrid blood.

MEGÆRA.
                  Her guile employs
The sweet soft shape of words of upper joys
More bitterly to rack his soul.

ALECTO.
                      Ha, sister,
The embrace!

TISIPHONE.
            She conquers.

MEGÆRA.
            He hath moved.

ALECTO.
　　　　　　　　　　　　　He hath kissed her!

TISIPHONE.
Ha! the worse hate of hate in love's white dress.

MEGÆRA.
And lewdness tricked to look like loveliness.

ALECTO.
Uttermost pain in pleasure's hour supreme.

MEGÆRA.
Hate's nightmare waking love's unreal dream.

ALECTO.
Claws, teeth, and poison!

TISIPHONE.
　　　　　　　　　　　　How she plies her pest!

MEGÆRA.
Strangling she holds him.

ALECTO.
　　　　　　　　　　　　In the inmost breast
Her hands defile him.

TISIPHONE.
　　　　　　　　　　　　In his rotting brain
He teeth, her breath, pass all imagined pain.

MEGÆRA.
Sisters!

ALECTO.
　　　We conquer!

TISIPHONE.
　　　Have we power?

MEGÆRA.
　　　　　　　　　　　　　　　The king
Endures, and is not moved at anything.

ALECTO.
He will not now relent.

TISIPHONE.
　　　　　　　　　　　　He's ours for ever!

HADES.
Ai! Ai!

MEGÆRA.
Hark!

ALECTO.
Listen!

TISIPHONE.
Now he yields -- or never!

HADES.
Release! Relent!

ECHIDNA.
Fair lover, let my embrace
Still gladden thee to rapture! let my face
Be like a garden of fresh flowers to cull,
And all thy being and thy body full
As mine of gentle love -- then sink to sleep!

MEGÆRA.
Ha! Ha! She mocks him! In the utter deep,
Her house of evil, sleep is stranger there.

ALECTO.
She sings!

TISIPHONE.
The final misery! Beware!

ECHIDNA.
O tender lover!
My wings still cover
  Thy face, and my lips
Are on thine, and my tresses
  Like Zephyr's caresses
When the twilight dips.

HADES.
This passes all. Relent. Release! Depart!
I yield: my power is broken, and my heart
Riven, and all my pride ruined, and me
Compelled to earth to loose Eurydice.

ORPHEUS.
Depart!

ERINYES.
Baffled! O misery! Bethink,
Proud Hades, ere thy torture gar thee drink

Humiliation's utmost dregs!

HADES.

I spake.
Depart ye! lest my power regained awake,
And smite ye with a terror more than ye.

MEGÆRA.

We are borne on bitter winds.

ALECTO.

We sink.

TISIPHONE.

We flee!

MEGÆRA.

To the abyss!

ALECTO.

Descend!

TISIPHONE.

Nor hope in vain
The ill-hearted one shall feel our fangs again.

MEGÆRA.

Murder and violation, deafened ear
To suppliants, these our friends are.

ALECTO.

Hate and fear
Leave not for long that bosom.

TISIPHONE.

Now away!
Back from this night more splendid than our day!

MEGÆRA.

We may not drag him down this chance.

ALECTO.

Despair
Not, O my sisters!

TISIPHONE.

The next suppliant's prayer
Rejected --

MEGÆRA.

Come, my sisters, we'll be there.

HADES.

Well, be it so. O wizard, by this strength
Thou hast availed in deepest Hell at length.
I grant thy prayer. Eurydice be given
To the sweet light and pleasant air of heaven!
Even on this wise. With Hermes for a guide
Up the dread steeps there followeth thee thy bride,
And thou before them singing. If thou yearn
Towards her, if thy purpose change or turn
While in these realms; if thou thy face revert;
That shall be hostage unto me for hurt
Of further magic: she shall fade and flee
A phantom frail throughout Eternity,
Driven on my winds, adrift upon my seas!
These are thy favours, and thy duties these.
Invoke thou Hermes, and thy lyre restring!

ORPHEUS.
This I accept and this shall be, O king!

[Invoking HERMES.]

O Light in light! O flashing wings of fire!
  The swiftest of the moments of the sea
    Is unto thee
  Even as some slow-foot Eternity
With limbs that drag and wheels that tire.
O subtle-minded flame of amber gyre,
  It seems a spark of gold
  Grown purple, and behold!
    A flame of gray!
  Then the dark night-wings glow
  With iridescent indigo,
    Shot with some violet ray;
And all the vision flame across the horizon
    The millionth of no time -- and when we say:
    Hail! -- Thou art gone!

The moon is dark beside thy crown; the Sun
  Seems a pale image of thy body bare;
    And for thine hair
  Flash comets lustrous with the dewfall rare
Of tears of that most memorable One,
The radiant Queen, the veiled Paphian.
  The wings of light divine
  Beneath thy body shine;
    The invisible
  Rayed with some tangible flame,
  Seeking to formulate a name,
    A citadel;
And the winged heels are fiery with enormous speed,
  On spurning heaven; the other trampling hell;

Orpheus

    And thou -- recede!

O Hermes! Messenger of inmost thought!
  Descent! Abide! Swift coursing in my veins
  Shoot dazzling pains,
The word of Selfhood integrate of Nought,
The Ineffable Amen! the Wonder wrought.
  Bring death if life exceed!
  Bid thy pale Hermit bleed,
    Yet Life exude;
  And wisdom and the Word of Him
Drench the mute mind grown dim
  With quietude!
Fix thy sharp lightnings in my night! My spirit free!
  Mix with my breath and life and name thy mood
    And self of Thee.

                      [HERMES *appears*: ORPHEUS *departs.*

The magical task and the labour is ended;
  The toils are unwoven, the battle is done;
My lover comes back to my arms, to the splendid
  Abyss of the air and abode of the sun.
The sword be assuaged, and the bow be unbended!
  The labour is past, and the victory won.

The arrows of song through Hell cease to hurtle.
  Away to the passionate gardens of Greece,
Where the thrush is awake, and the voice of the turtle
  Is soft in the amorous places of peace,
And the tamarisk groves and the olive and myrtle
  Stir ever with love and content and release.

O bountiful bowers and O beautiful gardens!
  O isles in the azure Ionian deep!
Ere ripens the sun, ere the spring-wind hardens
  Your fruits once again ye shall have me to keep.
The sleep-god laments, and the love goddess pardons,
  When love at the last sinks unweary to sleep.

The green-hearted hours shall burst into flowers.
  The winds shall waft roses from uttermost Ind.
Our nuptial dowers shall be birds in our bowers,
  Our couches the delicate heaps of the wind.
Where the lily-bloom showers all its light, and the powers
  Of earth in our twinning are wedded and twinned.

So singing I make reverence and retire;
Not with high words of worship fairly flung
To that sad monarch from the magic lyre,

And half the triumphs in my heart unsung,
Surpassing, as such triumphs must, all praise

Aleister Crowley

Of golden strings and human-fashioned tongue.

But now I follow the uprising ways
By secret paths indubitably drawn
Straight from the centre of the trackless maze

To light of earth and beauty of the dawn,
A sure swift passage taught of wit divine
To the wide ocean, the Achæan lawn.

For, wit ye well, not easy is that shrine
Of access to the mortal, as some tell,
Not knowing: easy and exact the line

Of light to upper air: but awful spell
And dire demand the inward journey needs:
That is the labour, that the work: for Hell

Is not designed for men's aspiring deeds.
The air is fatal, and the fear unspanned,
Even ere the traveller fronts the Stygian meads

And utmost edge of the detested land.
Wherefore already doth the light appear
Shaped in the image of a little hand

Far up the rocky cavern: warm and clear
The good air sends its fragrance: glory then
To the great work accomplished even here,

Promise and purpose unto little men
Bound in life's limits: death indeed I sever
By will's efficiency and speechless ken

Of power not God's but man's. Forget this never,
O mortals chained in life's detested den!
I leave this heritage to you for ever.

  O light of Apollo!
   O joy of the sky!
  We see thee, we follow,
   We draw to thee nigh.
  We see thee unclouded,
   Whose hearts have been thinned,
  Whose souls have been shrouded,
   Whose ears are bedinned
  By hell's clamour. How did
   The strength that has sinned
  Avail in the crowded
   Abodes of the wind?

  By lightning of rapture
   The soul of my song

Orpheus

My love doth recapture;
 Lead up to the long
Years in blithe measure
 Of summer and ease;
Linger at leisure
 For passion and peace.
Sadness and pleasure
 Relent and release: --
A torrent, a treasure,
 A garden of Greece!

Selene, our sister,
 Our lover and friend,
Thy light hath long missed her:
 That hour hath an end.
All aeons to squander
 We chance at our will:
We may woo, work or wander
 Through time to our fill,
Hither or yonder
 By fountain or hill,
Each day growing fonder,
 Each night growing still!

Bright Hermes behind me
 Caduceus-armed
Guides: shall he blind me?
 My spirit be charmed?
The song shall not swerve her,
 Its glory shall shed
Respite, deserve her
 From gulfs of the dead.
Ah me! let it nerve her
 These conduits to tread
That lead to the fervour
 Of earth overhead!

Fire, thou dear splendour
 Of uppermost space,
Turn to me tender
 Thine emerald face!
Thy rubies be blended
 With diamond light!
Thy sapphires be splendid,
 Extended to sight!
The portals be rended
 That govern the night,
And the guardians bended
 To magical might!

O air of the glorious
 Garb of the globe,
Don thy victorious

Glittering robe!
The sun is before us;
    The moon is above.
Rise and adore us
    Ye dwellers thereof!
The Muses restore us
    To Greece: as we move
Swell the wild chorus
    Of welcome and love!

Alas! that ever the dark place
    Should from its rocky base
Give up no echo of the god's strong stride,
    And no one whisper steal and thrill
    My heart, dissolve the ill
That gathers close and fears me for my bride.

I were no worse if I were blind.
I may not look behind
to catch one glimpse of the dear face that follows,
    Lest I should gain forbidden lore
    And wisdom's dangerous store
Of the black secrets of those heights and hollows.

Alas! the way is over long,
    And weary of my song
I sing who yearn to catch my love, and hold
    In such ten-thousandfold caress
    As shall annul distress,
And from the iron hours bring the years of gold.

Alas! my soul is filled with fear,
    Is the hard conquest here?
Where is Eurydice? The god hath faded
    Back to invisible abodes
    And on these rocky roads
Comes no deep perfume of her hair light-braided.

Alas! I listen! and no breath
    Assures the walls of death
That life remembers, that their hate is quelled.
    My ears, my scent avail me nought;
    My slavish eyes are brought
By the command wherewith I am compelled.

Alas! my heart sinks momently.
    Fear steals and misery.
From faith in faith of Hell my thoughts dissever.
    Yet, O my heart! abide, endure!
    Seek not by sight to assure,
Or she is lost to thee and lost for ever!

Now breathes the night-air o'er the deep,

Orpheus

  And limb-dissolving sleep
Laps my own country, and the maiden moon
  Gleams silver barley from the sea,
  And binds it royally
Into a sheaf that waves to the wind's tune.

  The rocky portals rise above.
  Here I may clasp my love,
Here Hermes shall deliver. Ah! how shook
  Yon cliff at the wind's ardent kiss!
  This is the hour of bliss --
The sea! The sea! Eurydice! Look, Look!

  Ai! but like wind-whirled flowers of frost
  The flying form is lost!
Cancelled and empty of Eurydice
  The black paths where she trod!
  Ai! Ai! My God! My God!
Apollo, why hast thou forsaken me?

EXPLICIT LIBER TERTIUS

Aleister Crowley

LIBER QUARTUS VEL MORTIS

TO

MY WIFE

LYSANDER (*reads*).

"The riot of the tipsy Bacchanals
Tearing the Thracian singer in their rage."

THESEUS.

That is an old device.
Midsummer Night's Dream.

What could the Muse herself that Orpheus bore
The Muse herself, for her enchanting son
Whom universal Nature did lament
When by the rout that made the hideous roar
His gory body down the stream was sent
Down the swift Hebrus to the Lesbian shore?
Lycidas.

A brighter Hellas rears its mountains
  From waves serener far;
A new Peneus rolls his fountains
  Against the morning star.
Where fairer Tempes bloom, there sleep
Young Cyclads on a sunnier deep.
  .   .   .   .   .   .
Another Orpheus sings again
And loves, and weeps, and dies.
Hellas.

MOUNT IDA.

THE COMPANY OF THE MÆNADS.

MÆNADS.

Evoe! Evoe Ho! Iacche! Iacche!

Hail, O Dionysus! Hail!
  Winged son of Semelé!
Hail, O Hail! The stars are pale.
  Hidden the moonlight in the vale;
  Hidden the sunlight in the sea.

Blessed is her happy lot
  Who beholdeth God; who moves
Mighty-souled without a spot,

Mingling in the godly rout
  Of the many mystic loves.

Holy maidens, duly weave
  Dances for the mighty mother!
Bacchanal to Bacchus cleave!
Wave his narthex wand, and leave
  Earthy joys to earth to smother!

Io! Evoe! Sisters, mingle
  In the choir, the dance, the revel!
He divine, the Spirit single,
He in every vein shall tingle.
  Sense and sorrow to the devil!

Mingle in the laughing measure,
  Hand and lip to breast and thigh!
In enthusiastic pleasure
Grasp the solitary treasure!
  Laughs the untiring ecstasy!

Sisters! Sisters! Raise your voices
  In the inspired divine delight!
Now the sun sets; now the choice is
Who rebels or who rejoices,
  Murmuring to the mystic night.

Io! Evoe! Circle splendid!
  Dance, ye maids serene and subtle!
Clotho's task is fairly ended.
Atropos, thy power is rended!
  Ho, Lachesis! ply thy shuttle!

Weave the human dance together
  With the life of rocks and trees!
Let the blue delirious weather
Bind all spirits in one tether,
  Overwhelming ecstasies!

Io Evoe! I faint, I fall,
  Swoon in purple light; the grape
Drowns my spirit in its thrall.
Love me, love me over all,
  Spirit in the spirit shape!

All is one! I murmur. Distant
  Sounds the shout, Evoe, Evoe!
Evoe, Iacche! Soft, insistent
Like to echo's voice persistent: --
  Hail! Agave! Autonoe!

AGAVE.

Evoe Ho! Iacche! Hail, O Hail!

Praise him! What dreams are these?

                AUTONOE.

                                    Sisters, O sisters!

                AGAVE.
Say, are our brethren of the rocks awake?

                AUTONOE.
The lion roars.

                MÆNADS.

                                    O listen to the snake!

                AUTONOE.
Evoe Ho! Give me to drink!

                AGAVE.

                                    Run wild!
Mountain and mountain let us leap upon
Like tigers on their prey!

                MÆNADS.

                                  Crush, crush the world!

                AGAVE.
Tread earth as 'twere a winepress!

                AUTONOE.

                                    Drink its blood,
The sweet red wine!

                MÆNADS.

                            Ay, drink the old earth dry!

                AGAVE.
Squeeze the last drops out till the frame collapse
Like an old wineskin!

                AUTONOE.

                                So the sooner sup
Among the stars!

                AGAVE.

                        The swift, swift stars!

                MÆNADS.

                                        O night!
Night, night, fall deep and sure!

                AUTONOE.

                        Fall soft and sweet!

                    Orpheus

                    AGAVE.
Moaning for love the woods lie.

                   AUTONOE.
                                        Sad the land
Lies thirsty for our kisses.

                   MÆNADS.
                                        All wild things
Yearn towards the kiss that ends in blood.

                    AGAVE.
                                        Blood! Blood!
Bring wine! Ha! Bromius, Bromius!

                   MÆNADS.
                                        Come, sweet God,
Come forth and lie with us!

                   AUTONOE.
                                        Us, maidens now
And then and ever afterwards!

                    AGAVE.
                                        Chaste, chaste!
Our madness hath no touch of bitterness,
No taste of foulness in the morning mouth.

                   AUTONOE.
O mouth of ripe red sunny grapes! God! God!
Evoe! Dwell! Abide!

                    AGAVE.
                                        I feel the wings
Of love, of mystery; they waft soft streams
Of night air to my heated breast and brow.

                   MÆNADS.
He comes! He comes!

                    AGAVE.
                                Silence, O girls, and peace!
The God's most holy presence asks the hymn
The solemn hymn, the hymn of agony,
Lest in the air of glory that surrounds
The child of Semelé we lose the earth
And corporal presence of the Zeus-begot.

                   AUTONOE.
Yea, sisters, raise the chant of riot! Lift

Your wine-sweet voices, move your wine-stained limbs
In joyful invocation!

MÆNADS.
Ay, we sing.

Hail, child of Semelé!
  To her as unto thee
Be reverence, be deity, be immortality!

Shame! treachery of the spouse
  Of the Olympian house,
Hera! thy grim device against the sweet carouse!

Lo! in red roar and flame
  Did Zeus descend! What claim
To feel the immortal fire had then the Theban dame!

Caught in that fiery wave
  Her love and life she gave
With one last kissing cry the unborn child to save.

And thou, O Zeus, the sire
  Of Bromius -- hunger dire! --
Didst snatch the unborn babe from that Olympian fire:

In thine own thigh most holy
  That offspring melancholy
Didst hide, didst feed, on light, ambrosia, and moly.

Ay! and with serpent hair
  And limbs divinely fair
Didst thou, Dionysus, leap forth to the nectar air!

Ay! thus the dreams of fate
  We dare commemorate,
Twining in lovesome curls the spoil of mate and mate.

O Dionysus, hear!
  Be close, be quick, be near,
Whispering enchanted words in every curving ear!

O Dionysus, start
  As the Apollonian dart!
Bury thy horned head in every bleeding heart!

AGAVE.
He is here! He is here!

AUTONOE.
Tigers, appear!

AGAVE.

To the clap of my hand
And the whish of my wand,
Obey!

AUTONOE.

I have found
A chariot crowned
With ivy and vine,
And the laurel divine,
And the clustering smell
Of the sage asphodel,
And the Dædal flower
Of the Cretan bower;
Dittany's force,
And larkspur's love,
And blossoms of gorse
Around and above.

AGAVE.

The tiger and panther
Are here at my cry.
Ho, girls! Span there
Their sides!

MÆNADS.

Here am I!
And I! We are ready.

AGAVE.

Strong now and steady!

FIRST MÆNAD.

The tiger is harnessed.

SECOND MÆNAD.

The nightingale urges
Our toil from her far nest.

THIRD MÆNAD.

Ionian surges
Roar back to our chant.

FOURTH MÆNAD.

Aha! for the taunt
Of Theban sages
Is lost, lost, lost!
The wine that enrages
Our life is enforced.
We dare them and daunt.

AGAVE.

The spirits that haunt
The rocks and the river,
The moors and the woods,
The fields and the floods,
Are with us for ever!

MÆNADS.

Are of us for ever.
Evoe! Evoe

AUTONOE.

Agave! He cometh!

AGAVE.

Cry ho! Autonoe!

ALL.

Ho! Ho! Evoe Ho! Iacche! Evoe! Evoe!
  The white air hummeth
  With force of the spirit.
  We are heirs: we inherit.
  Our joys are as theirs;
  Weave with you prayers
  The joys of a kiss!
  Ho! for the bliss
  Of the cup and the rod.
    He cometh! O lover!
  O friend and O God,
    Cover us, cover
    Our faces, and hover
  Above us, within us!
    Daintily shod,
    Daintily robed,
  His witcheries spin us
  A web of desire.
  Subtle as fire
  He cometh among us.
    The whole sky globed
    Is on fire with delight,
  Delight that hath stung us,
    The passion of night.
  Night be our mistress!
  That trees and this tress
  Weave with thy wind
  Into curls deep-vined!
    Passionate bliss!
  Rapture on rapture!
  Our hymns recapture
    The Bromian kiss.
  Blessed our souls!
    Blessed this even!

    We reach to the goals
      Of the starriest heaven.
Daphnis, and Atthis, and Chrysis, and Chloe,
Mingle, O maidens! Evoe! Evoe!

DIONYSUS.

  I bring ye wine from above,
    From the vats of the storied sun;
  For every one of ye love,
    And life for every one.
Ye shall dance on hill and level;
    Ye shall sing in hollow and height
In the festal mystical revel,
    The rapturous Bacchanal rite!
The rocks and trees are yours,
    And the waters under the hill,
By the might of that which endures,
    The holy heaven of will!
I kindle a flame like a torrent
    To rush from star to star;
Your hair as a comet's horrent,
    Ye shall see things as they are!
I lift the mask of matter;
    I open the heart of man;
For I am of force to shatter
    The cast that hideth -- Pan!
Your loves shall lap up slaughter,
    And dabbled with roses of blood
Each desperate darling daughter
    Shall swim in the fervid flood.
I bring ye laughter and tears,
    The kisses that foam and bleed,
The joys of a million years,
    The flowers that bear no seed.
My life is bitter and sterile,
    Its flame is a wandering star.
Ye shall pass in pleasure and peril
    Across the mystical bar
That is set for wrath and weeping
    Against the children of earth;
But ye in singing and sleeping
    Shall pass in measure and mirth!
I lift my wand and wave you
    Through hill to hill of delight:
My rosy rivers lave you
    In innermost lustral light
I lead you, lord of the maze,
    In the darkness free of the sun;
In spite of the spite that is day's
    We are wed, we are wild, we are one!

FIRST MÆNAD.

O sweet soul of the waters! Chase me not!

Aleister Crowley

What would'st thou!

A VOICE AS OF RUNNING BROOKS.
Love!

FIRST MÆNAD.
Love, love, I give, I give.
I yield, I pant, I fall upon thy breast,
O sacred soul of water. Kiss, ah kiss,
With gentle waves like lips my breast, my two small breasts,
Rose flames on ivory seas!

SECOND MÆNAD.
Nay! Nay! O soul
Of ivy, clingst thou so for love?

A VOICE AS OF THE RUSTLING OF IVY.
For love.

SECOND MÆNAD.
Cling not so close! O no! cling closer then!
Let thy green coolness twine about my limbs
And still the raving blood: or closer yet,
And link about my neck, and kill me so!

THIRD MÆNAD.
Soul of the rock! Dost love me?

A VOICE AS OF FALLING ROCK.
I love thee.

THIRD MÆNAD.
Woo me then!
Let all the sharp hard spikes of crystal dart,
Press hard upon my body! O, I fall,
Fall from thy crags, still clinging, clinging so,
Into the dark. Oblivion!

A DISTANT VOICE.
Io Evoe!
[ORPHEUS *enters.*

CROWD OF MÆNADS.
Evoe! Evoe! It is a lion!

FOURTH MAÆNAD.
Lion,

Orpheus

O lion, dost thou love?

FIFTH MÆNAD.
Thee I love,

O tawny king of these deep glades!

SIXTH MÆNAD.
What wood

Were worthy for thy dwelling?

CHORUS.
Come, come, come,

O lion, and revel in our band!

ORPHEUS.
Alas!

I sorrow, seeing ye rejoice.

FIRST MÆNAD.
O lion!

That is not kind.

ORPHEUS.
    Too kind. Since all is sorrow,
Sorrow implicit in the purest joy,
Sorrow the cause of sorrow; evil still
Fertile, and sterile love and righteousness.
Eurydice, Eurydice!

SECOND MÆNAD.
Drink wine!

ORPHEUS.
Ay, mask the grisly head of things that are
By drowning sense. Such horror as is hid
In life no man dare look upon. Woe! Woe!

AGAVE.
Call then reproach upon these maiden rites!

ORPHEUS.
Nay! virtue is the devil's name for vice,
And all your righteousness is filthy rags
Wherein ye strut, and hide the one base thought.
To mask the truth, to worship, to forget;
These three are one.

AGAVE.
What art thou then? a man?

ORPHEUS.

No more.

AGAVE.

No longer?

ORPHEUS.

Nothing.

AGAVE.

What then here
Dost thou amid these sacred woods?

ORPHEUS.

I weep.

AGAVE.

Weep then red wine!

AUTONOE.

Or we will draw thy tears,
Red tears of blood.

AGAVE.

On girls! this bitter fool
Would stop our revel!

ORPHEUS.

Nay! ye bid me cease
Weeping.

AGAVE.

Then listen! drink this deep full cup,
Or here we tear thee limb from limb!

ORPHEUS.

Do so!
Ay, me! I am Orpheus, poor lost fool of Fate!
Orpheus, can charm the wildest to my lyre.
Beasts, rocks, obey -- ah, Hades, didst thou mock,
Alone of all, my songs? Thee I praise not.

[AUTONOE *embraces him.*

Audacious woman!

AGAVE.

Tear the fool in shreds!
Then to the dance!

ORPHEUS.

The old Egyptian spell!

Orpheus

Stir, then, poor children, if ye can! Ah me!

[*Sings.*

  Unity uttermost showed,
   I adore the might of thy breath,
  Supreme and terrible God
   Who makest the Gods and death
     To tremble before thee: --
     I, I adore thee!

O Hawk of gold with power enwalled,
Whose face is like an emerald;
Whose crown is indigo as night;
 Smaragdine snakes about thy brow
Twine, and the disc of flaming light
 Is on thee, seated in the prow
Of the Sun's bark, enthroned above
With lapis-lazuli for love
 And ruby for enormous force
Chosen to seat thee, thee girt round
With leopard's pell, and golden sound
 Of planets choral in their course!
O thou self-formulated sire!
Self-master of thy dam's desire!
Thine eyes blaze forth with fiery light'
 Thine heart a secret sun of flame!
I adore the insuperable might:
 I bow before the unspoken Name.

For I am Yesterday, and I
 To-day, and I to-morrow, born
Now and again, on high, on high
 Travelling on Dian's naked horn!
I am the Soul that doth create
 The Gods, and all the Kin of Breath.
I come from the sequestered state;
 My birth is from the House of Death.

Hail! ye twin hawks high pinnacled
 That watch upon the universe!
Ye that the bier of God beheld!
 That bore it onwards, ministers
Of peace within the House of Wrath,
Servants of him that cometh forth
At dawn with many-coloured lights
 Mounting from underneath the North,
The shrine of the celestial Heights!

He is in me, and I in Him!
 Mine is the crystal radiance
That filleth æther to the brim
 Wherein all stars and suns may dance.
I am the beautiful and glad,
 Rejoicing in the golden day.

Aleister Crowley

I am the spirit silken-clad
  That fareth on the fiery way.
I have escaped from Him, whose eyes
  Are close at eventide, and wise
To drag thee to the House of Wrong: --
I am armed! I am armed! I am strong! I am strong!
I make my way: opposing horns
  Of secret foemen push their lust
In vain: my song their fury scorns;
  They sink, they grovel in the dust.

Hail, self-created Lord of Night!
Inscrutable and infinite!
  Let Orpheus journey forth to see
  The Disk in peace and victory!
Let him adore the splendid sight,
  The radiance of the Heaven of Nu;
Soar like a bird, laved by the light,
  To pierce the far eternal blue!

Hail! Hermes! thou the wands of ill
  Hast touched with strength, and they are shivered!
The way is open unto will!
  The pregnant Goddess is delivered!

Happy, yea, happy! happy is he
  That hath looked forth upon the Bier
  That goeth to the House of Rest!
His heart is lit with melody;
  Peace in his house is master of fear;
  His holy Name is in the West
When the sun sinks, and royal rays
Of moonrise flash across the day's!

I have risen! I have risen! as a mighty hawk of gold!
From the golden egg I gather, and my wings the world enfold.
I alight in mighty splendour from the throned boats of light;
Companies of Spirits follow me; adore the Lords of Night.
Yea, with gladness did they paean, bowing low before my car,
In my ears their homage echoed from the sunrise to the star.
I have risen! I am gathered as a lovely hawk of gold,
I the first-born of the Mother in her ecstasy of old.
Lo! I come to face the dweller in the sacred snake of Khem;
Come to face the Babe and Lion, come to measure force with them!
Ah! these locks flow down, a river, as the earth's before the Sun,
As the earth's before the sunset, and the God and I are One.
I who entered in a Fool, gain the God by clean endeavour;
I am shaped as men and women, fair for ever and for ever.

(*The* MÆNADS *stand silent and quiet.*)

ORPHEUS.
Worship with due rite, orderly attire,

Orpheus

The makers of the world, the floating souls
Whence fell these crystals we call earth. Praise Might
The Limitless; praise Pallas, by whose Wisdom
The One became divided. Praise ye Him,
Chronos, from whom, the third, is form perceived.
Praise ye Poseidon, his productive power,
And Juno, secret nature of all things,
On which all things are builded: praise ye Love,
Idalian Aphrodite, strong as fair,
Strong not to loosen Godhead's crown by deed
To blind eyes not a God's: and praise pure Life,
Apollo in his splendour, whom I praise
Most, being his, and this song his, and his
All my desire and all my life, and all
My love, albeit he hath forsaken me.
These are One God in many: praise ye Him!

AGAVE.

We praise indeed who made the choral world
And stars the greatest, and all these the least
Flowers at our feet: but also we may praise
This Dionysus, lord of life and joy,
In whom we may perceive a subtle world
Hidden behind this masquerade of things.
O sisters, hither, thither!

ORPHEUS.
       All deceit.

Delusive as this world of shadows is,
That subtler world is more delusive yet,
Involving deeper and still deeper: thought,
Desire of life, in that warm atmosphere
Spring up and blossom new, rank poisonous flowers,
The enemies of peace. Nay! matter's all,
And all is sorrow. Therefore not to be,
Not to think, love, know, contemplate, exist;
This Not is the one hope.

AGAVE.
       Believe it not!

Here is true joy -- the woodland revellings,
The smile, the kiss, the laughter leaping up,
And music inward, musings multiform,
Manifold, multitudinous, involved
Each in the deep bliss of the other's love; --
Ay me! my sisters. Thither!

AUTONOE.
       Wake the dance!

MÆNADS.
Pour luscious wine, cool, sweet, strong wine! Bring life,

Aleister Crowley

Life overflowing from the cup!

ORPHEUS.

Hush! Hush!

I hymn the eternal matter, absolute,
Divided, chaos, formless frame of force,
Wheels of the luminous reach of space that men
Know by the name of Pan.

MÆNADS.

Hail! Hail!

Pan! Son of Hermes! God of Arcady
And all wild woodlands!

ORPHEUS.

Neither Son, nor Sire,

Nor God: but he is all: all else in him
Is hidden: he the secret and the self
Shrined central in this orb of eyeless Fate,
Phantom, elusive, permanent. In all,
In spirit and in matter immanent,
He also is the all, and all is ill.
Three forms and functions hath the soul; the sea
Murmurs their names repeating: *Maris* call
The soul as it engendereth things below;
Neptune the soul that contemplateth things
Above; and *Ocean* as itself retracts
Itself into itself: choose ye of these!
But I hymn Pan. Awake, O lyre, awake!
As if it were for the last time, awake!

[*He sings.*

In the spring, in the loud lost places.
 In the groves of Arcadian green,
There are sounds and shadowy faces
 And strange things dimly seen.
Though the face of the springtide as grace is,
 The sown and the woodland demesne
Have a soul caught up in their spaces,
 Unkenned, and unclean!

It takes up the cry of the wind.
Its eyes with weeping are blind.
A strong hate whirls it behind
 As it flees for ever.
Mad, with the tokens of Fear;
Branded, and sad, without cheer;
Year after ghastly year,
 And it endeth never.

And this is the mystical stranger,
 The subtle Arcadian God

That lurks as for sorrow and danger,
  Yet rules all the earth with his rod.
Abiding in spirit and sense
  Through the manifold changes of man,
This soul is alone and intense
  And one -- He is Pan.

More subtle than mass as ye deem it
  He abides in the strife that is dust.
Than spirit more keen as ye dream it,
  He is laughter and loathing and lust.
He is all. Nature's agonies scream it;
  Her joys quire it clear; in the must
Of the vat is His shape in the steam.
  It is Fear, and Disgust.

For the spirit of all that is,
The light in the lover's kiss,
The shame and sorrow and bliss;
  They are all in Pan;
The inmost wheel of the wheels,
The feeling of all that feels,
The God and the knee that kneels,
  And the foolish man.

For Pan is the world above
  And the world that is hidden beneath;
He grins from the mask of love;
  His sword has a jewelled sheath.
What boots it a maiden to gird her?
  Her rape ere the aeons began
Was sure; in one roar of red murder
  She breaks: He is Pan.

He is strong to achieve, to forsake her;
  He is death as it clings to desire,
Ah, woe to the Earth! If he wake her,
  Air, water and spirit and fire
Rush in to uproot her and break her: --
  Yet he is the broken; the pyre,
And the flame and the victim; the maker,
  And master and sire!

And all that is, is force.
A fatal and witless course
It follows without remorse
  With never an aim.
Caught in the net we strive;
We ruin, and think we thrive;
And we die -- and remain alive: --
  And Pan is our name!

For the misery catches and winds us

Deep, deep in the endless coil;
Ourself is the cord that binds us,
  And ours is the selfsame toil.
We are; we are not; yet our date is
  An age, though each life be a span;
And ourself and our state and our fate is
  The Spirit of Pan.

O wild is the maiden that dances
  In the dim waned light of the moon!
Black stars are her myriad glances:
  Blue night is the infinite swoon!
But in other array advances
  The car of the holier tune;
And our one one chance is in mystical trances; --
  Thessalian boon!

For swift as the wheels may turn,
And fierce as the flames may burn,
The spirit of man may discern
  In the wheel of Will
A drag on the wheels of Fate,
A water the fires to abate,
A soul the soul to make straight.
  And bid "be still!"

But ye, ye invoke in your city
  And call on his name on the hill
The God who is born without pity,
  The horrible heart that is chill;
The secret corruption of ages
  Ye cling to, and hold as ye can,
And abandon the songs of the sages
  For Passion -- and Pan!

O thou heart of hate and inmost terror!
  O thou soul of subtle fear and lust!
Loathsome shape of infamy, thy mirror
  Shown as spirit or displayed as dust!
O thou worm in every soul of matter
  Crawling, feasting, rotting; slime of hell!
Beat and batter! shear and shatter!
  Break the egg that hides thee well!
Pan! I call thee! Pan! I see thee in thy whirling citadel.

I alone of all men may unveil thee,
  Show the ghastly soul of all that is
Unto them, that they themselves may hail thee,
  Festering corruption of thy kiss!
Thou the soul of God! the soul of demon!
  Soul of matter, soul of man!
Show the gross fools, thine, that think them freemen,
  What thou art, and what thy heart,

And what they are, that they are thee,
  All creation, whole and part,
  Thine and thee, near and far: --
  Come! I call thee, I who can.
  Pan! I know thee! Pan! I show thee!
    Burst thy coffin open, Pan!

What have I said? What have I done?

MÆNADS.
Pan! Pan!

Evoe, Iacche! Pan!

AGAVE.
The victim!

AUTONOE.
Rend

The sole pure thing in this impure gross lump,
The shapeless, formless horror that is us
And God -- Ah! rend him limb from limb!

ORPHEUS.
Apollo!

This is the night. This is the end of all.
No force detains. No power urges on.
I am free! Alas! alas! -- Eurydice!

(He is torn to pieces. A faint voice – like his -- is still heard, ever receding and failing.)

O night!
Fade, love! Fade, light!
I pass beyond Life's law.
I melt as snow; as ice I thaw;
As mist I dissipate: I am borne, I draw
Through chasms in the mountains: stormy gusts
Of ancient sorrows and forgotten lusts
Bear me along: they touch me not: I waste
The memory of long lives interlaced
Fades in my fading. I disintegrate,
Fall into black oblivion of Fate.
My being divides: I have forgot my name.
I am blown out as a thin subtle flame.
I am no more.

A SPIRIT.
What is? what chorus swells

Through these dark gorges and untrodden dells!
What whisper through the forest? Far entwines
The low song with the roses and the vines,
The high song with the mountains and the pines,
The inmost song with secret fibre of light,

And in the boiling pools and quorns and chasms
Chases the stryges, Death's devote phantasms,
Into a brilliant air wherein they are lost.
Deep in the river moans the choral roar,
Till the deep murmur of the Lesbian shore
Washed of the luminous sea gives answer, while
The angry wail of Nature doth beguile
The hours, the wrath of Nature reft of one,
The sole strong spirit that was Nature's sun,
The orb she circled round, the one thing clean
From all her gross machinery, obscene
And helpless: -- and the lonely mother-cry,
The Muse, her hope down-stricken. Magically
The full deep chorus stirs the sky;
Hark! one voice beyond all
Gives love's own call,
Not hers, Eurydice's,
But thine, thou sweet blood-breasted nightingale
Waking thy choral wail
From Mitylene to remotest seas!

THE RIVER HEBRUS.
Was e'er a stream before
So sad a burden bore
Rolling a melancholy sorrow down from shore to shore?

CALLIOPE.
O this is bitterness beyond belief.
Grief beyond grief.
Boots it to weep? I holp him not with force:
What should avail -- remorse?

RIVER HEBRUS.
Hear upon high the melancholy
Antistrophe
Matching the strophe's agony!
Tides on a terrible sea!

CALLIOPE.
Bear, bear the laurelled head
Of him I loved, him dead,
O Hebrus, ever downward on thy bosom iron-red!

RIVER HEBRUS.
All Nature's tunes are dull.
The beautiful,
The harmony of life is null.

CALLIOPE.
What unto us remains

But in these broken strains
To hymn with voices jarred the jarred world's shriek of woe?

O! O!

RIVER HEBRUS.
This discord is an agony
Shuddering harsh in me;
My waters will empoison the fair fresh-water sea!

CALLIOPE.
Nay! all is ended now.
Cover the beaten brow!
Carry the brain of music into the wide Ægean!
No priest pronounce thy paean
Ever again, Apollo,
Thou false, thou fair, thou hollow!
Die to a groan within a shrine!
Despair thy force divine!
Thou didst achieve this ruin; let the seas
Roar o'er thy lost name of Musagetes!

THE LESBIAN SHORE.
Welcome, O holy head!
Welcome, O force not dead!
Reverberating joy of music subtly shed!
Welcome, O glorious, O laurelled one!
Own offspring of the Sun,
The ancient harmony was hardly yet begun.
By thee and by thy life
Arose the Lesbian maiden.
Thou art perished as thy wife;
My shores with magic loves and songs of life are laden.

CALLIOPE.
Weep, weep no more!
O loyal Lesbian shore,
I hear a murmur sound more sweet than murmur ever bore.
Not ocean's siren spell
Soft-sounded in a spiral shell
Were quite so exquisite, were all so admirable!

LESBIAN SHORE.
Nay! but the agony of the time
Rings in the royal rime!
She hath touched the intimate, and chanced on the sublime.

CALLIOPE.
Ay! Ay! a woman's silky tone
Makes music for eternity her own,
Till all men's victories in song seem a discordant groan.

LESBIAN SHORE.

Upon my cliffs of green,
Beneath the azure skies,
She stands with looks of fire,
Sappho. Her hands between
Lies the wild world; she flies
From agony to agony of desire.

CALLIOPE.

Him, Orpheus, him she sings;
Loosing the living strings,
Till music fledged fares forth sunward on moon-wrought wings.

LESBIAN SHORE.

Yea, by the solar name,
Orpheus her lips acclaim,
The centre and the silence! O! the torrent of fine flame
   Like hair that shooteth forth
   To the ensanguine North
Whence ran the drunken crew, Bassarids in their wrath.

SAPPHO.

Woe is me! the brow of a brazen morning
Breaks in blood on water athirst of Hebrus.
Sanguine horror starts on her hills tenebrous:
   Hell hath not heard her!

Dumb and still thy birds, O Apollo, scorning
Song; yells drown them, lecherous anthems gabbled,
Laughter splashed of Bassarids, blood-be-dabbled,
   Mad with their murder!

O thou many-coloured immortal maiden,
Dawn! O dew, delight of a world! A sorrow
Hides your holy faces awhile. To-morrow
   Comes for your calling?

Still the notes of musical Orpheus, laden
Never now of pain or of failing, follow;
Follow up the height, or adown the hollow
   Fairy are falling.

O my hopeless misery mind of longing!
O the anguish born in a breast unlovered!
Women, wail the face of a God uncovered,
   Brain dead and breath dumb!

Wail the sense of infinite ardours thronging
Fast and fast and faster athwart the heaven,
Keen as light and cruel as fire, as levin
   Swift and as death dumb!

Freedom, rapture, victory, fill the chorus,

Orpheus

Dying, ever dying, among the billows;
Whispered, ever whispered among the willows: --
    Pour the libation!

Now springs up a notable age. Adore us
Masters now of music above his magic,
Lords of change, leaps pastoral up to tragic,
    Thanks to the Thracian!

Ah, my pain! what desolate female bosoms,
Smitten hearts of delicate males, uncover;
Grip not life for poet or sage or lover,
    Feed on derision.

Yea, in these mature me avenger blossoms
Swift as swords to sever the subtle ether,
Lift the earth, see infinite space beneath her,
    Swoon at the vision.

This, O Orpheus, this be a golden guerdon
Unto thee for gift of amaze and wonder!
This thy sorrow, sword of a heart asunder,
    Beareth a flower.

This the heart of woman -- a bitter burden! --
Thou has filled with seed -- O a seed of madness!
Seed of music! seed of a royal sadness! --
    This be our dower!

Ah! the bitter legacy left of lyre-light!
Thou wast Nature's prophet, a wise magician;
Magic fails, and love is a false physician: --
    Deep our disease is!

Now to us the crouching over the firelight,
Eating out for hunger of love our vitals!
(Eaten out the hollower for respitals
    Swift as the breeze is.)

Ay! the golden age is a broken vessel.
All the golden waters exhale, evanish.
Joy of life and laughter of love we banish:
    Damned is the will dead.

Now with brass and iron we writhe and wrestle.
Now with clay the torrent of fire is tainted.
Life apes death: the lily is curled and painted;
    Gold is regilded.

Master, we lament thee, as awful anguish
Seizes on the infinite maze of mortals.
See we love that yearns to the golden portals
    Bound of the grey god.

Love, thy children, laughter and sunlight, languish.
Aphrodite, miracle of the flashed foam,
Burns with beaten agony in the lashed foam;
    Down is the day-god.

Ay! this first of Lesbian lamentations
Still shall burn from aeon to idle æon!
(Chorus, epithany, ode, and paean
    Dumb or dishevelled!)

Still my songs shall murmur across the nations,
Gain their meed of misery, praise, and yearning,
Smite their stroke on centuries foully burning,
    Drunk or bedevilled.

Song? No beauty shine in a sphere of music!
Me? my voice be dull, be a void, be toneless!
Match me, sea! than me thou hast many a moan less,
    Many a million!

Sun, be broken! Moon, be eclipsed; be dew sick!
Ocean flat and poisonous, earth demented!
Living souls go shuddering through the tented
    Air, his pavilion!

Ay; the pectis clangs me a soulless discord: --
Let me break my visible heart a-weeping!
Loving? Drinking? Misery. Singing, sleeping
    Touch not my sorrow.

Orpheus, turn the sorrow-chord to the bliss-chord!
All may rise the easier that the one set.
So our eyes from saddening at the sunset
    Turn to to-morrow.

CALLIOPE.

    Silence. I hear a voice
    That biddeth me rejoice.
    I know the whole wise plan
    Of fate regarding Man.

THE LESBIAN SHORE.

It is the sun's dark bride
Nuith, the azure-eyed.
No longer Sappho sings her spell;
His heart divorced, her heart insatiable.
There is deep silence. Earth hath passed
To a new kingdom. In a purpose vast
Her horoscope is cast.

NUITH.

    Enough. it is ended, the story

Orpheus

Of magical aeons of song;
The sun is gone down in his glory
To the Houses of Hate and of Wrong.
  Would ye see if he rise?
  In Hesperian skies
Ye may look for his rising for long.

The magical aeon beginneth
Of song in the heart of desire,
That smiteth and striveth and sinneth,
But burns up the soul of the lyre: --
  There is pain in the note: --
  In the sorcerer's throat
Is a sword, and his brain is afire!

Long after (to men: but a moment
To me in my mansion of rest)
Is a sundawn to blaze what the glow meant
Seen long after death in the west;
  A magical æon!
  Nor love-song nor pæan,
But a flame with a silvery crest.

There shall rise a sweet song of the soul
  Far deeper than love or distress;
Beyond mortals and gods shall it roll;
  It shall find me, and crave, and caress.
    Ah! me it shall capture
    In torrents of rapture;
  It shall flood me, and fill, and possess.

For brighter from age unto age
  The weary old world shall renew
Its life at the lips of the sage,
  Its love at the lips of the dew.
    With kisses and tears
    The return of the years
Is sure as the starlight is true.

Yet the drift of the stars is to beauty,
  To strength, and to infinite pleasure.
The toil and the worship and duty
  Shall turn them to laughter and leisure.
    Were the world understood
    Ye would see it was good,
A dance to a delicate measure.

Ye fools, interweaving in passion.
  The lyrical light of the mind!
Go on, in your drivelling fashion!
  Ye shall surely seek long and not find.
    From without ye may see
    All the beauty of me,

And my lips, that their kisses are kind.

For Eurydice once I lamented;
For Orpheus I do not lament:
Her days were a span, and demented;
His days are for aye, and content.
  Mere love is as nought
  To the love that is Thought,
And idea is more than event.

O lovers! O poets! O masters
Of me, ye may ravish my frown!
Aloof from my shocks and disasters!
Impatient to kiss me, and crown!
  I am eager to yield.
  In the warrior field
Ye shall fight me, and fasten me down.

O poets! O masters! O lovers!
Sweet souls of the strength of the sun!
The couch of eternity covers
Our loves, and our dreams are as done.
  Reality closes
  Our life into roses;
We are infinite space: we are one.

There is one that hath sought me and found me
In the heart of the sand and the snow:
He hath caught me, and held me, and bound me,
In the lands where no flower may grow.
  His voice is a spell,
  Hath enchanted me well!
I am his, did I will it or no.

But I will it, I will it, I will it!
His speck of a soul in its cars
Shall lift up immensity! fill it
With light of his lyrical bars.
  His soul shall concentre
  All space; he shall enter
The beautiful land of the stars.

He shall know me eternally wedded
To the splendid and subtle of mind;
For the pious, the arrogant-headed,
He shall know they nor seek me nor find.
  O afloat in me curled!
  Cry aloud to the world
That I and my kisses are kind!

O lover! O poet! O maiden
To me in my magical way!
Be thy songs with the wilderness laden!

Thy lure be adrift and astray: --
  So to me thou shalt cling!
  So to me thou shalt sing
Of the beautiful law of the day!

I forbid thee to weep or to worship;
  I forbid thee to sing or to write!
The Star-Goddess guideth us her ship;
  The sails belly out with the light.
    Beautiful head!
    We will sing on our bed
  Of the beautiful law of the Night!

We are lulled by the whirr of the stars;
  We are fanned by the whisper, the wind;
We are locked in the unbreakable bars,
  The love of the spirit and mind.
    The infinite powers
    Of rapture are ours;
  We are one, and our kisses are kind.

EXPLICIT LIBER QUARTUS

Printed in Great Britain
by Amazon